KEEPING
GOOD
LAWYERS

Best Practices to
Create
Career Satisfaction

M. Diane Vogt
Lori-Ann Rickard

Law Practice Management Section
American Bar Association
Defending Liberty
Pursuing Justice

Commitment to Quality: The Law Practice Management Section is committed to quality in our publications. Our authors are experienced practitioners in their fields. Prior to publication, the contents of all our books are rigorously reviewed by experts to ensure the highest quality product and presentation. Because we are committed to serving our readers' needs, we welcome your feedback on how we can improve future editions of this book. We invite you to fill out and return the comment card at the back of this book.

Cover design by Emily Friel.

Nothing contained in this book is to be considered as the rendering of legal advice for specific cases, and readers are responsible for obtaining such advice from their own legal counsel. This book and any forms and agreements herein are intended for educational and informational purposes only.

The products and services mentioned in this publication are under or may be under trademark or service mark protection. Product and service names and terms are used throughout only in an editorial fashion, to the benefit of the product manufacturer or service provider, with no intention of infringement. Use of a product or service name or term in this publication should not be regarded as affecting the validity of any trademark or service mark.

The Section of Law Practice Management, American Bar Association, offers an educational program for lawyers in practice. Books and other materials are published in furtherance of that program. Authors and editors of publications may express their own legal interpretations and opinions, which are not necessarily those of either the American Bar Association or the Section of Law Practice Management unless adopted pursuant to the bylaws of the Association. The opinions expressed do not reflect in any way a position of the Section or the American Bar Association.

Library of Congress Catalog Card Number 00–132768
ISBN 1–57073–793–2

04 03 02 01 00   5 4 3 2 1

Discounts are available for books ordered in bulk. Special consideration is given to state bars, CLE programs, and other bar-related organizations. Inquire at Book Publishing, American Bar Association, 750 N. Lake Shore Drive, Chicago, Illinois 60611.

ACKNOWLEDGMENTS

Every book is a community project, and this one is certainly no exception. We would like to acknowledge and thank everyone who helped us with interviews, informal conversations, advice, and guidance. We would also like to thank our friends and colleagues who gave us their unflagging support and encouragement in this project.

Our families, who gave so generously of their time to make it possible for us to work on the book and who supported us at every step of the process, are part of all that we do every day. Neither our legal careers nor this book would have become a reality without them.

Our staff—Linda Lee, Bill Smoak, Lisa Caruso, Mike Caruso, and Karla Kongieser—has provided countless contributions, for which we would like to make our appreciation public. Last, but certainly not least, we appreciate the assistance of Howard Hatoff, Beverly Loder, Angela Kelly, and Tim Johnson.

CONTENTS

PART ONE
Lawyers and the Profession

Recognition of lawyer value, job satisfaction, and retention of lawyers who are engaged in the practice will increase client base, secure client loyalty, make the practice more profitable and more likely to prosper.

CHAPTER 1

> *Every night, an organization's most important assets walk out the door and go home. In today's marketplace, more than capital assets or real estate, the most valuable thing a business has is its intellect: good old American know-how. A law firm epitomizes that structure. A law firm or department is only as good as its lawyers. The goal of every individual lawyer is to be "difficult to replace/high value added."*

CHAPTER 2

> *A lawyer is called to the profession. The lawyer's desire, skill, and dedication are the very essence of who the lawyer is. Yet, that calling, like any other talent, must be nurtured, supported, and respected.*

CHAPTER 3

> *Free agency is a concept that has come to apply to all "knowledge workers," and most especially lawyers. This presents a challenge to law practices that must be addressed and understood because lawyers are not just intellectual capital; they are the practice's only real asset.*

CHAPTER 4

General Dissatisfaction and Malaise

After five or more years of practice, legal work often loses its luster and life seems so much more satisfying anywhere else. It's often "the conflict" that causes the most dissatisfaction, although conflict resolution is the sine qua non of lawyering. A successful practice is built by a voluntary association of lawyers with a common goal or mission.

CHAPTER 5

The Brain Drain

Experienced lawyers are leaving their practices and, in some cases, the profession. This trend results, in part, from an unproductive view of lawyers, their jobs, and their roles in society.

CHAPTER 6

Culture and Personal Style

Culture may be the most significant issue facing law practices today. Many practices don't know what their culture is, nor how to blend a lawyer's personal style or lateral hires into the existing culture. Resolving style or culture dissonance may make more of a difference in retention and job satisfaction than any other single issue.

——————— PART TWO ———————
Learning and Change

Solutions are easier to articulate than to implement. Solutions require an ability to change and adapt to the current business environment, a commitment to the concepts, and a willingness to assist and allow lawyers to develop to their full potential.

CHAPTER 7

Best Practices: How to Attract, Train, and Retain Best Lawyers

Fairly concrete steps can be taken to achieve improvement in retaining the best lawyers in various stages of practice, regardless of the size of the organization.

CHAPTER 8

Best Lawyers: Career Design and Career Building

To improve personal job satisfaction, lawyers must be vigilant in taking charge of personal career development at every stage of practice.

CHAPTER 14

Innovation   77

Lawyers and practices must engage their right-brain thinking, be flexible, and learn to manage their practices in creative ways. Consider that it might be possible to think differently than you do now.

CHAPTER 15

Generation X   83

Managing Generation X presents its own challenges, but those challenges are equally present in Baby Boomers. The résumé building and learning characteristics of Generation Xers supply creative management solutions for all lawyers.

CHAPTER 16

Abundance of Graduates   87

Graduating significant numbers of lawyers, many of whom have difficulty finding jobs out of school, does not mean that we will have a large number of productive partners in our law firms ten years hence. Indeed, associate attrition statistics and the declining population suggest just the opposite.

CHAPTER 17

Finders, Binders, Minders, Grinders   91

Practices should recognize that all four types of lawyers are necessary to make the firm productive and profitable. Focusing on finders will ensure the firm has plenty of work. Ignoring the other categories will ensure dissension, dissatisfied clients, and reduced production capacity. Developing plans to value and retain binders, minders, and grinders will enhance the practice. Recognize that the top-of-the-pyramid partners may no longer have the client control the firm assigns to them. A minder, who is often viewed as dispensable, is the true client contact and the lawyer the client views as "mine."

CHAPTER 18

Variable Compensation Systems   95

Address compensation with flexibility to accommodate all types of individual lawyers and their needs. Elements of fairness, value, and the "going rate" (that is, the rate that keeps the lawyer from going) must be addressed and perceived as appropriate by the lawyers themselves.

CHAPTER 19

Recruiting and Delivery of Promises 103

Many lawyers report feeling that they were misled during the recruiting process. Lawyers make an effort to identify their concerns and address them when they take new positions. If the recruiting process is not scrupulously honest, buyer's remorse decreases loyalty and increases attrition, with the commensurate loss of expertise and revenue.

CHAPTER 20

Make Good Hiring Decisions 107

Hire lawyers whose goals and aspirations can be met by the practice and who will enhance the practice by their presence.

CHAPTER 21

Profit Centers 113

Recognition of existing profit centers and creation of additional ones will make the lawyer more valuable to the firm, increase individual value, and encourage engagement. Training in marketing the individual and the firm will benefit all concerned.

CHAPTER 22

Mentoring to Increase Satisfaction 117

Apprenticeship, training, support, and general enhancement of lawyer value are all essential, but only if the lawyer is committed to becoming a productive partner of the practice. Firm partners should publicize the reasons the firm is an excellent place to work, and should encourage retention.

CHAPTER 23

Understand Practice Goals 121

Are partners attempting to build a firm that will be valuable to its clients, the profession, and future generations of lawyers? Or, is the practice a group of lawyers intending to provide jobs for themselves as long as they wish to practice? Identifying the goal of the practice will dictate many of its activities and policies.

CHAPTER 24

Honest Appraisal and Evaluation 127

This process must be value driven to ensure and inspire trust, without which a practice cannot flourish.

CHAPTER 25

Recognize and Eliminate Lawyer Dissatisfaction   **131**

Every lawyer leaves the practice because of some dissatisfaction with the firm. This is true even in circumstances when the lawyer is accepting a "better opportunity," following a spouse to another city, or moving from private practice into government service. If the lawyer was satisfied with the firm, she would not quit.

CHAPTER 26

Perception Is Reality   **135**

Recognize that management's perception of events, just because it is based on different and often superior knowledge, is not the same as the perception of other lawyers in the firm. Unless lawyers communicate with management regularly and openly, management has no way of knowing the perception of certain events "in the trenches." Yet that knowledge is essential. The only way to get it is to seek the information.

CHAPTER 27

Be Proactive   **141**

It's not enough to know what lawyers want; Best Practices also do something about it. Use the information you gather to improve the practice.

CHAPTER 28

Apply the Platinum Rule   **145**

Treat lawyers not just the way management believes is fair, but the way the lawyers themselves believe is fair. A satisfied lawyer will stay with the firm longer and lend her considerable talents to the firm for their mutual benefit.

--------------------- PART THREE ---------------------
Separate Gracefully

When separation is inevitable, separate gracefully. This is the time to create or solidify a marketing opportunity. Every lawyer has alumni potential. The relationship between the firm and every lawyer should last a lifetime.

CHAPTER 29

Best Practices Separate Gracefully   **153**

Techniques exist for fostering cooperative, lucrative, and lasting business relationships with lawyers who leave your practice, regardless of the size of your organization.

INTRODUCTION

We began this project to test our hypothesis that "Happy Lawyer" is not an oxymoron. The aim of this book is to assist law practices in lawyer retention efforts by focusing on the need to improve job satisfaction for individual lawyers, as well as to help individual lawyers in their quest for the perfect practice. In the end, every lawyer is a solo practitioner making an independent decision about where or whether to practice law today. Successful lawyer retention by law practices and the profession is directly related to the individual lawyer's decision to continue to volunteer his or her talents. Like players on a sports team, members of a legal team are "the talent." Lawyers are the most important asset the team has. On the flip side, a great sportsperson is of no consequence without a team that allows the individual to showcase his or her talents and perform to full potential. The relationship between the player, the team, and the game is mutually beneficial. Unlike sports teams, however, most organizations do not pay lawyers giant-sized salaries, or provide them with personal trainers, several coaches, lots of opportunity for practice before the big game, media attention, and fans for adulation. For that matter, most practices don't even give lawyers employment contracts. Every day, a lawyer is left to decide whether the lawyer's current association is best for him or her, and many practices are not even aware that the question is on the floor.

Our work with lawyer retention and improving job satisfaction for lawyers has shown us how pervasive lawyer dissatisfaction is, and how much the profession needs to address this issue. For example, a recent survey of the Michigan bar reflected that 47 percent of lawyers were dissatisfied and 83 percent thought about issues related to stress and burnout at least once a month. Lawyers often like the work, but don't like their jobs. Law firms that are addressing "inclusion" and "diversity" have focused on attracting top talent and clients. There is relatively little focus on improving job satisfaction to keep lawyers in their jobs once the firm has attracted them.

Lawyers, like people generally, have a desire to be happy and to live balanced lives. That balance, though, is perceived to be unattainable. Lawyers perceive that being dissatisfied with the practice is just the nature of being a lawyer and that nothing can be done to change it. Reading the title of this book, one forty-two-year lawyer told us: *"If you can figure out a way to [improve job satisfaction] you'll sell a million copies."* This level of hopelessness is particularly disturbing to us.

The relationship between job satisfaction and lawyer retention is, it seems to us, obvious. Yet generally, the profession, lawyers, and managers of lawyers place very little emphasis on improving job satisfaction or keeping lawyers in the practice. Part of the reason for this lack of attention to job satisfaction has been the idea that the practice of law is a privilege that everyone wants, but is reserved for those who pass the various forms of "trial by fire" that we use these days to license and regulate lawyers. Many also hold the view that there are too many lawyers already, so if lawyers become dissatisfied with their practices and turn to other pursuits, so much the better. In many organizations lawyers are treated like commodities—as interchangeable as chairs. A managing partner told his partners, "Associates are fungible goods." Indeed, there is an anti-lawyer sentiment in America that is manifested daily in derisive commentary and lawyer bashing.

There is something of the martyr in lawyers as well. Law practice carries mostly financial rewards and occasional victories when lawyers actually get to help people and make a difference. But for the most part, lawyers believe the practice is hard, tedious, consuming, serious, important, and thankless work that they are constrained to do because someone has to do it and, goodness knows, the people can't do it for themselves. The suggestion that the practice of law should be fun—and that lawyers are entitled to enjoy life and their work— is viewed as heresy. But, as author and motivational speaker John Powers said, "Sorrow finds us. It's fun we have to look for.

Lawyers also believe they are the fourth branch of government and feel that responsibility keenly. They take seriously that they are officers of the court, even as they walk ever closer to—and perhaps over—the ethical line in the name of advocacy. Unlike doctors, lawyers are not taught and have not learned the lessons of transference and detachment. Lawyers are protective of their clients and take on their clients' problems as their own. They are trained to think that by the time they argue a client's case, they should truly believe that their client's point of view is the only point of view. Lawyers volunteer their time and their talents to help those less fortunate than themselves, partly because most states require them to do so, but mostly because they want to give something back to their communities. Lawyers make great sacrifices of time, money, and family to their work. They resent—rightfully so—the public's poor perception of lawyers and increasingly demand that their national, state, and local bar associations do something about improving that perception, beyond more rigid self-policing.

Chief among the reasons for lawyer dissatisfaction are the "golden hand-cuffs." Many lawyers told us that they continue to practice law because it pays better than anything else they can do and they have certain financial needs that can be met only by continuing to make their current levels of income, or more. Financial expectations are high among lawyers, and there is a certain amount of denial about how financially successful lawyers are in comparison with other Americans. For example, though many American families of four live on $25,000 a year, single lawyers have trouble accepting salaries of twice that amount. The U.S. Bureau of Labor Statistics reported that the median weekly wage of all Americans in 1998 was $523, but for judges the median was $1,290, or more than twice the national median. Judges are about average in the compensation level of all lawyers, and many lawyers in private practice make substantially more. Lawyers also have a disturbing tendency to live beyond their means and to engage in subtle forms of self-sabotage in money matters.

Research for this book has included interviews of law students, aspiring lawyers, judges, government lawyers, law firm partners, solo and small-firm practitioners, house counsel, associates, lawyers working with the "Big 5" accounting firms, consultants, and lawyers who have left the profession to work in both law-related and nonlegal jobs. All the lawyers with whom we've talked have spoken to us candidly, in response to our express promise that we would respect the confidentiality of their communications. We have changed certain identifying characteristics to protect identity, and we have made no effort to quote lawyers precisely, choosing instead to attempt to convey intent more than exact words. Nor have we attempted to conduct an empirical study with statistically significant results, although other organizations we identify in the book have done so in areas that we believe are relevant to the issues we've addressed.

Despite the "nonscientific" scope of our project, what we've reported here are the common themes lawyers experience. We have experienced them ourselves, our friends and colleagues have experienced them, and experts we've consulted, volumes we've reviewed, and meetings we've attended have addressed them as well. Indeed, the issues we discuss are nearly universal in legal life. It is not our intent to persuade the skeptics with data. Instead, we aim to share information with those who are interested, and who want to change rather than give up and leave either present jobs or the profession entirely.

Speaking regularly with lawyers involved in all aspects of the practice has given us a great deal of insight on a variety of issues reflecting the relationship between lawyer retention and job satisfaction. We have become convinced that the most satisfied lawyers are the ones most practices most want to keep: the "A players," the lawyers who are "high value added/hard to replace" or what we call "Best Lawyers." Devoting firm resources to coaching and developing lawyers will result not only in greater lawyer satisfaction, but also greater firm success, lawyer retention, and client loyalty. Although associate training is available in most firms, it generally focuses on substantive legal training and rarely includes concepts of professionalism, client tending, civility, the bounds of advocacy, life balance, career design, career challenges, and similar topics. Many firms have in-house "universities" to assist lawyers with fulfilling their continuing legal education requirements. Again, the focus here is on the group and not the individual. Thus, most lawyer organizations—whether firms, departments, or agencies—do little to nurture and engage their talent, particularly at the senior level. Those that seek such goals we call "Best Practices."

Recognizing that a law practice develops in certain fairly well-defined stages is the first step in designing a career that will be successful for the individual lawyer. A successful, fun, rewarding, and challenging legal career is within the grasp of every lawyer and can be had without fleeing either the practice or a current association; but it takes planning and diligence.

We believe all law practices should aim to be Best Practices, include only the Best Lawyers, and provide their lawyers the means to become such lawyers.

When every lawyer is satisfied and believes his or her current association is the best one, lawyer retention will no longer be a problem.

We have struggled to develop our own successful careers. Through our own process of trial and error and developing successful, satisfying practices for ourselves, we became convinced that the way most lawyers view their jobs and the profession is responsible for a great deal of dissatisfaction, burnout, and attrition from organizational practice and the profession. PeopleWealth's retention consulting practice was created and developed after many, many lawyers told us of their struggles to find satisfaction in the practice. This struggle often lasts for years and results in resignation—to the futility of the struggle or from the profession all together.

Our personal success and work in career building have taught us that "Happy Lawyer" is not an oxymoron. Our hope is that this book will assist individual lawyers and law practices to understand the issues and focus on improving job satisfaction for lawyers. We believe that the time has come to realize the concept of the satisfied, happy lawyer. We sincerely hope that the ideas and strategies in this book will effect change, improve job satisfaction for lawyers, and keep qualified lawyers enthusiastically serving the public.

LAWYERS AND THE PROFESSION

Recognition of lawyer value, job satisfaction, and retention of lawyers who are engaged in the practice will increase client base, secure client loyalty, make the practice more profitable and more likely to prosper.

In this section, we endeavor to create some common ground as we explore the concepts that explain the current state of the legal profession and its relationship with lawyers. Most law practices have come to realize that associate retention is an economic necessity. Retention efforts are beginning to focus on keeping junior lawyers to increase gross revenues and help with the workload, particularly with the declining population. Fledgling retention efforts have not focused on improving job satisfaction for senior lawyers or, more important, on self-preservation for practices and the profession.

However, a law practice depends on loyal clients and client loyalty is dependent on lawyers. Lawyers develop the personal relationships with decision makers who form the third and most significant level of the marketing process: bringing the business in the door and keeping it there. Clients place legal work with lawyers they know and trust, and with whom they have developed relationships. When lawyers leave, clients go, too.

In law practices, lawyers write the firm's newsletters and supervise the work of the support staff. Lawyers draft the documents, conduct the negotiations, argue the cases. They do the training, recruiting, and mentoring of the practice's future producers. They are the marketing, production, billing, and collection departments. Without lawyers, there are no practices.

Lawyers want to enjoy their work and find meaning in what they do. Cynics accurately report that millions of people do work they don't like and millions more are unhappy at work. But today's lawyers are unwilling to practice law under less than ideal circumstances. Nor should they.

CHAPTER 1

INTELLECTUAL CAPITAL

Every night, an organization's most important assets walk out the door and go home. In today's marketplace, more than capital assets or real estate, the most valuable thing a business has is its intellect: good old American know-how. A law firm epitomizes that structure. A law firm or department is only as good as its lawyers. The goal of every individual lawyer is to be "difficult to replace/high value added."

Lawyers have always been knowledge workers in an economy that valued production of goods. Today, lawyers epitomize the intellectual-capital concept central to the information age. Thomas A. Stewart's book, *Intellectual Capital*, was published in 1997 following a series of articles on the same subject. Stewart is a member of the board of editors of *Fortune* magazine. His book, and others like it that appear fairly regularly in the business press, attempt to make sense of the "Information Age Economy" in which we live today, and to value the contribution workers make to a successful enterprise. Stewart's premise is that intellect is any business's most valuable asset.

The premise that knowledge and the people who possess it are the only indispensable asset of today's business cannot be seriously disputed. But regardless of the merits of Stewart's theories to business generally, they are axiomatic to law practice. The only things lawyers have to contribute to their practices and the world are their knowledge, training, and experience. Lawyers know how to figure things out. In thinking, we are the most useful we can be. We have no "product" beyond our ability to decipher the law and apply it to the particular circumstances in which our clients find themselves.

In corporate America, efforts have begun to count and place a value on the intellectual capital of a business. Estimates of four to sixteen times the tangible book value of the corporation have been postulated. The idea is that smart workers work smarter and are therefore a balance sheet asset. Intellectual capital is not the revenue generated by lawyers, which goes on the income statement. It is the value of the lawyer herself—just her presence on the firm's résumé. The concept is that a lawyer, by her mere presence, before she bills the first hour, has significant value to the firm.

Stewart notes that companies manage human capital haphazardly because they cannot distinguish between the cost of paying people and the value of investing in them. (Stewart at 85) Alas, this has also been true of law practices. As one law firm administrator told us: *"If they are unhappy, we want them to leave."* This is like saying, "If I have to change the oil or put gas in my car, I'd rather walk." By contrast, a "Big 5" accounting firm lawyer said this:

> *We want people to be happy and successful. If they can't be happy here, we want to place them somewhere they'll like better.*

In other words, it is the quality of unhappiness rather than the existence of dissatisfaction that should drive the decision to part company. Some things are easily and cheaply fixed.

Stewart argues that people in organizations fall into one of four categories: (1) difficult to replace, high value added, (2) difficult to replace, low value added, (3) easy to replace, high value added, and (4) easy to replace, low value added. (Stewart at 90) Those who fit in the first category are an asset. The rest are labor costs.

The challenge, then, for individual lawyers and for law practices, is to attract, hire, retain, and become those lawyers who are difficult to replace and add high value to the firm, or "Best Lawyers." To do this, what we call "Best Practices" first recognize the need to find such lawyers, define the characteristics they possess, develop them from the available talent pool, and nurture them once they are onboard.

Best Practices understand that all lawyers have the capacity to be Best Lawyers. Lawyers are, after all, some of the nation's "best and brightest." Lawyers have demonstrated that they have the capacity to learn what is well taught. Otherwise, they wouldn't have been admitted to law school in the first place, let alone graduated, passed the bar exam, and practiced law. Indeed, unlike medical school, there is little effort made to graduate lawyers who are admitted to law school. At least 35 percent of graduates fail the bar exam and are excluded from practicing law for that reason. In other words, once a piece of human capital eventually gets a license to practice law, it is at least a pretty safe bet that she has what it takes to become a Best Lawyer. If she doesn't make the cut, the reason is more likely training, experience, or motivation than lack of ability.

Best Practices ask not what the lawyers can do for the practice but what the practice can do for its lawyers. They recognize that every lawyer adds value to the practice and, if the practice has sold her properly, profits to the bottom line. The challenge is to keep the lawyer asset actively engaged and productive.

Most law practices have done nothing to quantify the value of each lawyer to the practice and thus do not know the value of their assets. Estimates on the cost of associate attrition run from $80,000 to over $275,000 per junior associate, assuming the associate is replaced within 90 to 120 days.[3] Partner attrition is much more costly. Most law office software now calculates work-in-progress as well as receivables and write-offs. Practices can easily track revenue by client, and record which lawyers work on each matter. Practices should also record the "soft costs" and "soft profits" of lawyers and other revenue generators to fully recognize lawyer value.

For example, how much time (which is what most firms count, for lack of a better method) did each lawyer spend in recruiting, mentoring, committee meetings, unbilled interoffice conferences, continuing legal education, and client development each year? What is the lost profit or opportunity cost of such time? What is the return on investment of that time?

By tracking such information and adding it to revenue generated, practices can value their intellectual capital and understand what they have as well as what they will lose with attrition. Looking at the revenue generated per lawyer by time billed or work generated for other lawyers as the sole basis for valuing contribution to the firm is self-defeating and demoralizing. A law practice cannot be kept alive by lawyers who make no contribution other than billing time or generating business, even if the economic reality is that making money is essential. When efforts are made to capture all costs, attrition costs several times higher than revenue generated are reflected. In 1999, at least three firms began offering retention bonuses of $40,000 or more to associates who stay with the firm at least four years, a move that surely reflects understanding of the value of retaining experienced lawyers.

Finally, a successful law practice is about more than money. It's about compatibility, rewarding work, camaraderie, service, and intellectual stimulation. But the notion that a law practice can be successful if it fails to appreciate and value its lawyers—allowing its talent to leave due to an idea that the firm is more important than the individuals who populate it or that lawyers are easily replaced—is simply wrong. Law firms close their doors every day. If you don't want yours to be next, you must properly appreciate, value, enhance and support your intellectual capital.

CHAPTER 2

LAW IS A VOCATION

A lawyer is called to the profession. The lawyer's desire, skill, and dedication are the very essence of who the lawyer is. Yet, that calling, like any other talent, must be nurtured, supported, and respected.

Lawyers are high achievers who have worked hard to get where they are, out of desire that is more than just an interest in money, power, or position. Lawyers we've interviewed tell us they want to help people and work directly with clients. They enjoy the intellectual challenge of the work. Lawyers feel they are serving society in a larger way than they could otherwise do as individuals. Often, they practice at great personal sacrifice. Many have been divorced several times, have serious and debilitating illnesses, put off life events such as having children or visiting elderly parents, and still persevere in the practice. In short, lawyers believe that they have been called to the profession—that it is their one true purpose in life.

In all jurisdictions, the lawyer's oath exacts promises of fealty, honesty, and piety, and rejects pure capitalism. The vocation is more than the oath. Many lawyers we interviewed are living examples of the calling. A successful mediator who previously practiced commercial litigation at a national firm recently applied for an appointment to a circuit court. The position she sought was in family law, an area in which she had little experience. Besides requiring her to learn the law, the job would certainly cap her income potential and restrict her personal freedom significantly. When we asked her why she wanted the job, she told us this:

I want the opportunity to make a difference. I made some significant new law when I was a young lawyer. Since then, I really haven't accomplished very much. I'll be fifty years old this year. I want my life to count for something and my daughter to be proud of me.

7

Another successful lawyer with a private practice in white-collar criminal defense for over fifteen years recently applied to be a federal public defender, a government job paying less money than she currently earns. She is a single parent:

> *I like the work I do. But I just feel that this would be a good next step for me, an opportunity to have a broader impact. I know I can do a good job.*

A lawyer who has practiced for nine years told us of her recent decision to join her firm's pro bono group:

> *I've applied to be the rotating lawyer in our firm's community services team. I didn't become a lawyer to make money. I became a lawyer to help people. If taking a couple of years away from my practice means I pay a client develop-ment price for that, it's a price I'm willing to pay.*

Explaining why she left her lucrative big-firm practice after three years to work for less money in a smaller plaintiffs' firm handling nursing-home abuse cases, a highly qualified and financially independent lawyer told us this:

> *Our firm is a specialized practice area that includes critical social/ public policy issues and exposure to a client base that I want to help, and that facilitates my desire to be civically active and make a contribution to my community.*

Surveys reflect that the most satisfied lawyers work for the government, either as judges or in the federal or local government systems. These lawyers are certainly not the highest paid members of our profession. When we inter-viewed them, they told us why they like the *work.* A lawyer in the appellate department of the U.S. Attorney's Office said it this way:

> *This is the best job in the world. What I'm doing is important. It matters.*

A county attorney's description of her job and the work she does was equally inspiring:

> *My work is varied and challenging. One day, I'm defending a sports fran-chise and the next day, I'm prosecuting the franchise. Lawyers in my office are not competitive with one another. We all work together to get the job done.*

The talent, desire, and dedication that leads one to become a lawyer is not extinguished by a lawyer's failure to thrive in law practice, but neither will a lawyer develop to his or her full potential without building on that base. The entry-level lawyer's highest and best use is to develop skills to create something or someone even more valuable to the lawyer, the practice, and society. The lawyer shouldn't have to struggle alone.

Nurturing the lawyer and developing his talent are ultimately the individ-ual lawyer's responsibility. But the organization with which the lawyer is affili-ated can benefit greatly by assisting in this development. Lawyers work in orga-nizations and associations because people enjoy working with others in a social and supportive environment. A woman who has practiced law for nine years, now in a large firm after working as a judicial clerk and also as a part-time, self-described "citizen activist," told us she recently went to her department head and asked for help with her workload:

> *I had been having a lot of fun in my practice for the past two years. But I had become overloaded—really stressed. And I wasn't having fun anymore. Work has to be fun for me. So I asked for help and they gave it to me. Otherwise, I would probably have quit.*

One large-firm partner recommended more firm social events to increase job satisfaction and decrease competition among partners:

> *These social events must not be work in disguise, though. If the participants perceive they are being tested in a social setting or forced to attend to advance their careers, social activities will simply be another arena for dissatisfaction to develop.*

Americans don't work primarily for money. Studies of lottery winners show that most return to work even when they have financial independence. Similarly, lawyers are called to the profession and the happiest lawyers remain in the pure practice of law without regard to compensation for their efforts.

The pro bono efforts of lawyers reflect our true values. A ten-year lawyer with a busy solo practice and a special-needs child told us why she devotes so much of her time to helping other families get medical benefits:

> *Most of them just don't know where to turn. They have no insurance coverage left, or at least their carriers won't pay for their child's needs. They certainly have no money to pay a lawyer. But they need help and I've had experience with it. I have to do what I can.*

Another senior solo lawyer told us why she devoted so much time (over a hundred hours in two months) to pro bono representation of abused children at great personal and professional sacrifice:

> *I just can't stand to see children abused or living in abusive situations. I can't let that happen without trying to do something about it.*

Yet, the calling doesn't have to result in successful law practice to serve the profession. A nine-year lawyer explained why she made the switch from private practice to legal recruiting:

> *I was a good lawyer. I liked the work. But it wasn't my calling. It wasn't everything to me. I love what I'm doing now. I feel I'm really contributing here. I'm really making a difference. I have an opportunity to change things.*

And a lawyer in practice for more than twenty years told us why she wanted to be president of the state bar:

> *I think I'm just an inveterate do-gooder. I want to help lawyers and I think it's time bar associations did that. Most people don't understand the obligations lawyers have to the judicial system and how the system relies on us as officers of the court. We need to improve our public image and let the public know what we really do.*

A "retired" lawyer in practice for forty years, who still comes in to the office every day and now devotes his time to service of the profession on the judicial qualifications commission, said this:

> *The purpose of the bar association is to improve the justice system. I've worked toward that goal all my life. If we improve the way the system works, we'll instill public confidence in lawyers.*

Lawyers are drawn to the law and they stay with it, in one form or another, for years after the need to make money is met. This intrinsic motivation is present to some degree in all lawyers. It should be recognized, nurtured, encouraged, and supported. Best Lawyers and Best Practices remind themselves that they are professionals, with a vocation, and do not get distracted from their true purpose.

CHAPTER 3

FREE AGENCY

Free agency is a concept that has come to apply to all "knowledge workers," and most especially lawyers. This presents a challenge to law practices that must be addressed and understood because lawyers are not just intellectual capital; they are the practice's only real asset.

Perhaps as never before, a good lawyer—though maybe not as valuable as Michael Jordan before he left basketball—is a hot commodity. This is due to a combination of factors: the growth of law firms and other legal employers, a client's willingness to "hire the lawyer, not the firm," increasing numbers of lawyers, rising costs, stagnant hourly rates, and the technology explosion that has leveled the playing field. A lawyer who has managed her financial affairs wisely can afford to listen to the best offers that come her way. Lawyers, too, have accepted the concept of "Me, Inc."

The death of loyalty has been bemoaned but is a fact of life. Business is not loyal to workers and workers have developed a portable survival response that is focused solely on the individual. For law practices the focus on employment at will as an attempt to avoid costly lawsuits has contributed to the demise of long-term work relationships. Large, impersonal, multi-office law practices also foster detachment. Lawyers today, like the population at large, are loyal to people with whom they work, not their large-practice employers. Lawyers will not sacrifice themselves "for the good of the firm."

Client loyalty is closely tied to lawyer loyalty. In this context, loyalty can be defined as a "commitment to the practice." To engender lawyer loyalty, practices must offer loyalty to their lawyers. Loyalty is a concept that is the antithesis of free agency. It suggests commitment on both sides to the practice. As long as firms and departments demonstrate no loyalty or commitment to lawyers, even the senior lawyers can and do feel free to demonstrate no loyalty or commitment to the practice.

11

Capital One, a credit card company, recently advertised its place as number forty-one on *Fortune* magazine's 1999 annual list of "100 Best Companies To Work For," in its January issue. Capital One advertises a list of benefits that make nirvana look like hell and with which most law firms don't even try to compete. For instance, Capital One provides all employees with medical, vision, and dental coverage starting the first day on the job, ten paid holidays, three family-care days, three weeks of vacation in the first year, paid child care (going out to find it for everyone who needs it), 401K plan, casual dress all week long, stock available for purchase at a 15-percent discount (meaning all employees can be "partners" at their sole discretion), and 100-percent tuition reimbursement. And, as if all that isn't enough, every manager has a quarterly "fun budget" to make sure work and play stay in balance.

Keep in mind, the *Fortune* list puts Capital One at number forty-one with all these attributes, even though 93 percent of the people who work for Capital One are happy with their benefits, 90 percent voted it a fun place to work, and 93 percent say they are proud to work there. This means there were *forty* companies that were *better* than Capital One on the list.

By contrast, there is only one law firm on the 1999 list, and it wasn't on the list in 1998. The one law firm listed has the least gross revenue of any of the companies on the list by almost half. The firm ranks substantially lower than any other service company listed. What does that say for all the law firms that didn't make it, or couldn't even apply? Lest you think being on this list is irrelevant, companies that make the list, on average, make two-and-a-half times more profit than unlisted companies.

The point of this story is to show that, in general, law firms are not the best places to work in America, and every member of every law firm can choose from a great number of alternative work environments that are regularly touted as "better." No one is chained to the desk. Good lawyers are needed everywhere and associates perceive that law firms "don't care about me." Lisa Imus, a lawyer and legal recruiter with Professional Placement Services, Inc., located in Tampa, Florida, has estimated that it takes less than six weeks for an associate to find a new job:

> *I've seen it happen in a matter of days. At the same time, it takes firms two to four months to replace an associate who's left, and then there's the learning curve after that.*

Many law firms are not in a financial position to offer the benefits an employee can get from corporate employers. But the argument can be made that law firms never will be able to offer such benefits if they don't grow their businesses. Growing a law business, or any service business, is not easy. But competitors at the "Big 5" accounting firms are doing it in a big way. Two "Big 5" firms that made the *Fortune* list employ over 4,000 lawyers each, making them substantially larger law practices than the nation's largest law firms.

Senior lawyers are often invested in their practices, both financially and emotionally. As "owners" of the enterprise, partners are theoretically responsible for the organization and its management. In reality, though, multi-office practices have a management team or partner and non-management partners serve at the will of management. Indeed, we recently heard about a large, multi-national firm that "let fifteen partners go." The reality that owners can lose their positions when management decides they are no longer wanted gives every lawyer the "Me, Inc." perspective.

A lawyer in his sixth year of practicing with only one associate, after previously practicing for thirteen years with two large national firms, told us how much more satisfied he is with his practice since he made the move:

> It used to be that the best lawyers were with the big firms. Now, the best lawyers are never there. It is a mistake to follow the accounting method of organization. We don't have a standardized product like they do. Litigation is not a group activity. I don't believe in pyramids of lawyers. I make as much money, or more, than I would make in the big firms. People ask me how I do it all. We don't do it all. We do what we think is necessary and we try to do everything right the first time.

Another lawyer who made the opposite change, from small firm to large, said this:

> I wanted to work with people who are more experienced than me. I'm not a manager and only want to practice law. I've enjoyed all my jobs. They all have benefits. I'm happy or I change it.

Law practices, and particularly law firms, can be better places to work than they currently are. Improving the practice will make some lawyers stick with a firm, even in the presence of a better offer from businesses or consulting firms. Lawyers will stay with a practice if they *want* to do so, and practices must make lawyers *want* to stay. Focusing on creative ways to retain lawyers, making a commitment to retention, and adopting a formal retention plan are the first steps.

It should be apparent that lawyers have many opportunities to work in environments where life is not as restrictive as it is in most firms. Lawyers are "free agents" today. One senior lawyer put it this way:

> Not every day is a good day. If they get a call from a headhunter on a bad day, they leave.

CHAPTER 4

GENERAL DISSATISFACTION AND MALAISE

After five or more years of practice, legal work often loses its luster and life seems so much more satisfying anywhere else. It's often "the conflict" that causes the most dissatisfaction, although conflict resolution is the sine qua non of lawyering. A successful practice is built by a voluntary association of lawyers with a common goal or mission.

Perhaps as early as the third year of law school, many law students have already decided that they've made the wrong career choice. We have been asked to speak at law schools and seminars on the subject of "alternative careers for lawyers," and because we are practicing lawyers ourselves, our consulting practice is sometimes viewed as an "alternative career." Most of the "alternatives" discussed at such meetings are careers in and around law practices that require or are enhanced by a law degree, such as lawyer recruiting and placement, contract legal work, teaching law, judicial clerkships, legal writing, state bar work, work at legal research companies, and so on.

One creative student, with two excellent traditional legal job offers, candidly told us he had decided to spend the summer after his last year in law school as a camp counselor for high-school kids, despite his parents' dismay at the apparent "waste" of his legal degree. Such a job clearly doesn't require a J.D., and he will be seriously underemployed. But senior lawyers who hear this story invariably say they think he's pursuing the right path and will be happier than if he were practicing law.

Seasoned practitioners tell us law practice is a difficult job that, as it is traditionally done, isn't particularly satisfying. The Michigan bar's 1999 Quality of Professional Life Survey reflected that 38 percent of lawyers are concerned about their quality of life and 47 percent are dissatisfied with the practice. After five to twenty-five years, many lawyers say they would gladly trade their jobs to be a camp counselor, novelist, or antique-store owner, but most continue to practice. In other words, seasoned practitioners want to encourage others to pursue their nonlegal passions, but don't do so themselves. An eighteen-year shareholder with a twenty-lawyer firm practicing civil litigation won a "best lawyer" award not long ago. He told us this:

> *Let's face it. What we do isn't intrinsically rewarding. But I have two small children. I'll have to do this a long time yet.*

Recently, a twenty-year partner at a litigation boutique firm went skiing in Utah with his family. On the third day of the vacation, he decided to "take the day off and do some business." Lawyers believe that one's practice is always beckoning. There is more to do than there is time to do it. Most lawyers say they take only about two weeks of vacation each year, and very rarely go on vacation without checking voice mail and responding to practice issues. Eighty-three percent of Michigan lawyers surveyed felt concerned at least once a month (and 36 percent at least once a week) about client expectations and pressure for productivity. One state's commission on attorney professionalism is considering a statewide policy for lawyer vacations as a way to make courtrooms more civil, as one of the factors in lack of civility seems to be lawyer stress levels due to overwork. Lawyers feel as though nothing can be done but to continue to practice until leaving the practice altogether or retiring early.

A fifty-three-year-old lawyer who has practiced for twenty years as a big firm partner told us:

> *One day I'm going to get on another hot airplane sitting on the boiling tarmac and I'm just going to give it up. I need to do this five more years and then I'm going to retire.*

Lawyers excited and energized by law practice who enjoy the work in the early years develop a feeling of general dissatisfaction at about the fifth year. A number of common themes arise in our conversations with lawyers on this point. Lack of respect from clients, colleagues, and society is one problem lawyers identify. Lawyers want to work with a practice that has a great reputation and with others who treat them as professional colleagues with a common goal. They want to feel valued and a part of a great team.

Personal growth is another issue lawyers seek after the routine challenges of the early years are mastered. Lawyers want to grow constantly. Their expectations are high and this doesn't end when they become partners. Senior lawyers get bored because they are doing repetitive work that no longer challenges them, either because the work is easy to get and easy to do, or because they have fallen into the habit of accepting whatever work comes their way.

After five years, lawyers still want to make money but they know money alone is not going to make them happy. Still, they feel they work hard. Economic security and earning a satisfactory living are major issues for lawyers, as they are for other Americans. If a practice doesn't provide a high level of pay and benefits, good people become dissatisfied. Most lawyers want to feel as though they work at a practice that is progressive and moves with the times.

Lawyers thrive in a practice that cares about their development and about them as people. Busy management and hard-working lawyers often leave little time for developing personal relationships between lawyers in a practice, resulting in emotional detachment and isolation. Most lawyers need mentors who help them learn during the various stages of practice. Some of these relationships are informally established, but the most successful practices formally assign all lawyers someone to mentor. Successful lawyers actively seek mentors. Properly done, the mentoring process goes a long way toward identifying individual dissatisfactions and creating those personal relationships that sustain engagement over the course of a career.

Lawyers receive little positive feedback from clients or management. Junior lawyers often feel stress, fearing their work inadequate because management provides no positive feedback. Often, management thinks lawyers are doing well, but no one bothers to tell the lawyers until they have already become dissatisfied and feel underappreciated. Senior lawyers are rarely shown appreciation, even for remarkable feats, because they are expected to know they aren't being taken for granted or because they are owners of the business and are expected to do well. But senior lawyers need appreciation, too. A fifteen-year lawyer commented:

> *It's always, "What have you done for me lately?" Every time I pull a rabbit out of the hat, they think there are two more in there.*

After acquiring certain levels of expertise so they feel more comfortable in their abilities, many lawyers become dissatisfied if they feel they do not fit in the firm's culture. A newer lawyer ahead of the curve told us this:

> *I've been practicing for three years, two as a judicial clerk and now one year with a firm. I don't know if I want to be a lawyer anymore. I don't like the long hours and I don't like the culture.*

One complaint that surprised us when it was first raised, considering that lawyers are in the conflict resolution business, was what individual lawyers called "too much conflict." In further interviews, we recognized the complaint as what the profession has been describing for a decade or more as lack of civility. This issue has been addressed by most state bars with educational programs and civility rules. However, these methods of increasing the civility with which lawyers do their jobs have not had a significant impact on those lawyers who are determined to behave too aggressively, which makes the practice unsatisfactory for many. A five-year lawyer told us why she left one large firm for another similar firm with a similar practice in the same building:

> *I probably could have gotten the same deal from my old firm, but I really wanted new cases to work on. I handled a lot of the same types of cases and the opposing counsel I worked with was just miserable. At least in the new job, I get someone new to deal with. I hope they'll be better.*

When we asked him whether he would do this work if he didn't get paid for it, a law firm partner in practice for fifteen years said:

Not a chance. I've been doing a lot of thinking about what I don't like about the practice and I think it's the conflict I don't like. I mean, there are some things that have to be resolved by the judge, but most of this stuff we could just agree to if both parties could be reasonable. Why does everything have to turn into such a pissing contest? It just ends up being more of a pain for everyone and I don't like it.

Both of these lawyers, and many more with whom we've spoken, intensely dislike the interpersonal conflict that develops in our adversarial system of justice. Best Lawyers have learned to deal appropriately with it, while still disliking the behavior in others. They recognize that the real conflict is between the parties and not the lawyers. They reject the view that the best representation for the client is to advocate the client's cause regardless of the client's interest in resolving the claim. Most clients want their cases resolved. Lawyers must respect that and not "fight to the death" over every issue. A widely respected senior real estate partner of a large law firm we interviewed told us:

There is too much conflict in my practice. When I started practicing law over twenty-five years ago, lawyers were respected and respectful of each other. Now, everyone just wants to argue over everything. I've already decreased my practice to three days a week and I'm planning to retire early.

Another twenty-year litigator said:

Part of the problem people have with the "conflict" issue is that they take everything so personally. Most of the time, the offending lawyer isn't attacking me personally. I understand that. I don't like it, but I know it's just advocacy and I don't get defensive about it either.

Lawyers benefit from training in interpersonal conflict resolution. Issues may separate the parties, but there is no reason for abusing counsel. Lawyers must behave appropriately themselves and then refuse to accept poor behavior by others. There is no reason why a lawyer should be subjected to or accept verbal or physical abuse. Simply announcing that the abuse will not be accepted, hanging up the phone, or walking away is usually all that is required. Confirming verbal agreements in writing avoids many disputes about content. Judges who enforce civility rules—instead of forever making the exception—are appreciated but rare. Lawyers who recognize that they are representing the client's cause and not their own understand there is no need to become personally aggressive.

Practices and lawyers must learn to deal with conflict in positive ways that do not allow a dispute to degenerate into personal stress. Leaving one's job or the profession because opposing counsel is violating all rules of civility is not a productive way to resolve this issue. Other solutions must be found and they must be effective. The profession has not been able to eradicate this behavior on a global scale in over ten years of trying. Wishing for a return to "the good old days" or limiting the number of lawyers is not the answer. Dissatisfaction and malaise are not inevitable, but rather, are the result of a failure to take proactive charge of one's career.

CHAPTER 5

THE BRAIN DRAIN

Experienced lawyers are leaving their practices and, in some cases, the profession. This trend results, in part, from an unproductive view of lawyers, their jobs, and their roles in society.

Although many people believe we have "too many lawyers," there is no question that our profession is suffering from the loss of legal talent—a "brain drain" of vast proportions. *Keeping the Keepers*, a recent study published by the National Association for Law Placement reported the high level of voluntary turnover among associates and junior partners in law firms. Every issue of bar publications announces lateral hires, new associations, practice mergers, and acquisitions. Hardly a week goes by when the average American newspaper fails to mention a "former lawyer" now involved in some new venture, and the fastest-growing "law firms" are the accounting and consulting practices. It seems that running from the law isn't just for criminals anymore.

Every time a lawyer leaves the firm or department, an irreplaceable capital asset is lost because a part of the firm's history, talent, training, and culture goes out the door with her. The lawyer's training and experience cannot be re-created because every lawyer is unique. Thus, it is a mistake to say that "replacement costs" can be calculated. Only the cost associated with finding another unique lawyer can be calculated. The lost lawyer, like a lost parent, can never be replaced.

When questioned about why they are leaving, lawyers explain that they like the work itself, but do not like the practice because they are not challenged and the work is boring and repetitive, the practice is too demanding or confining, or the price it exacts is not sufficiently rewarded. This desire to be a lawyer and the decision to leave the work create conflicts that are often irreconcilable. After leaving active practice, many lawyers come back to the work in a volunteer or pro bono capacity. The answer to job dissatisfaction is to improve the jobs we have, not to replace one unsatisfactory job with another. Like Dorothy, many lawyers travel to Oz only to discover there's no place like home could have been, if only they had realized the possibilities and made it so.

Many lawyers hold the view expressed by a twenty-five-year real estate lawyer with a very large firm, who described his plan to semi-retire at age fifty-five in two years:

> *I've talked to a lot of lawyers about job satisfaction. And you know what? It's not money. Most of us make plenty of money. People have tried working part-time, taking sabbaticals, the mommy track, big firm, small firm. It's all the same. You just can't be happy in the practice long term.*

On the contrary, many lawyers are happy in the practice for decades. Happy lawyers do exist and the main difference between the happy ones and those who are dissatisfied is a personal understanding of how to be satisfied. Law practices should teach this process because entry-level lawyers look ahead of them to senior professionals for role models and a glimpse of the future. A midlevel partner in private practice told us:

> *At one time, we had some problems and we addressed them. Now, our partners enjoy practicing together. The associates pick up on that and want to be part of it. We haven't had an associate leave in over two years and we haven't had a partner leave in five or six years. It seems to be working.*

When senior lawyers are either unsatisfied and say so or fail to recognize and vocalize their satisfaction, other lawyers form their own, often erroneous, conclusions about the state of the practice. Seniors are erroneously viewed as sad workaholics by juniors who recognize that workaholism is a block (not a building block), a substitute for life, and a coping mechanism that isolates one from life. It's become politically correct to praise balance, but most law practices still reward workaholism and many lawyers want more life in their lives. They think job hopping or leaving the profession will give them happiness.

A recent survey by *American Lawyer* magazine asked midlevel associates whether they planned to stay with their firms for two more years. Most said no. More than 3,000 associates were asked questions about their firms, such as the treatment they received from partners, the level of interesting work, training and guidance, atmosphere, management openness, emphasis on billables, attitudes toward pro bono, and whether information is adequately shared about "making partner." None of the law firms that were subject to the survey achieved even close to a perfect score.

The "making partner" question was also the subject of *Perceptions of Partnership* a 1999 National Association for Law Placement (NALP) study. This study reflected that many associates neither want to become partners nor believe partnership is within their grasp. The attitudes discovered by NALP led it to conclude that law firm partnerships are among the most endangered of American business forms.

The mounting evidence reflects that every lawyer wants to be happy and every practice should make the effort to help its lawyers achieve that goal.

Although research suggests that happy lawyers have a genetic predisposition to be happy, all lawyers can be happier by understanding basic goal-setting techniques, the elements of human happiness, and the antithetical training lawyers receive. Law practices can improve retention by understanding these issues and dealing with them.

There are nine basic elements of human happiness, best remembered by an acronym:

- **H**appy genes
- **A**ltruism
- **P**urpose in life
- **P**ositive attitude
- **I**ntimate relationships
- **N**ever retire
- **E**xercise
- **S**piritual life
- **S**mile

Lawyers are trained to think negatively. They analyze the risks in every situation presented by clients as a mechanism to devise appropriate safety nets. The longer lawyers continue in the practice and the more successful they are at doing it, the more they learn to see the potential downside of every situation. Although this thinking may make a successful lawyer, when it is transferred to other aspects of daily living it creates an atmosphere of negativity that is difficult to overcome. Simply understanding that professional thinking is the antithesis of happy thinking is a giant leap toward creating a more satisfactory practice.

A workaholic, according to *Webster's New Collegiate Dictionary*, is "a compulsive worker." The same source defines "burnout" as "the cessation of operation of a jet or rocket engine; the point at which burnout occurs." Lawyers seem particularly prone both to workaholism and burnout. After working long, hard hours for a certain amount of time, lawyers give up and get out of the practice—they cease to operate. Lawyers are also addicted to ambition, the insatiable desire to acquire more of everything just because success and achievements are such overwhelming facets of American culture in general, and law practice culture in particular.

Lawyers have difficulty with the issues of transference and detachment. They accept their clients' problems as their own. Unlike doctors, lawyers receive no training in methods to avoid overidentifying with clients. For lawyers who work on contingent fees, their economic gain is also tied to their clients' gain. In short, emotionally, lawyers cannot separate their clients' worlds from their own. The stress becomes overwhelming and they quit.

Lawyers in general are perceived by many as without ethics, as somewhat corrupt in their approach to their business, and as part of a profession that has a negative impact on society. One collector of jokes told us there are more "jokes" about lawyers than any other job, "jokes" that denigrate the profession. The public perception that lawyers are a drain on society perpetuates a view of lawyers that negatively impacts job satisfaction. Eighty-six percent of Michigan lawyers surveyed reported being concerned about the public image of the bar.

Lawyers are in a position to change this view. After passing the bar, and associating to practice in groups, lawyers often put other masters ahead of the calling and begin to serve instead money, ego, or pride. Changing public opinion requires constant public education and exemplary conduct by lawyers. Publicized cases involving lawyers who abuse the profession by taking advantage of a tragedy or by encouraging people to litigate instead of peacefully resolving their disputes further erode the public and private perception of lawyers. Over time these public images reduce personal and professional pride and contribute to the problem. Though the First Amendment guarantees lawyers the right to advertise and publicize their activities, the very act of speaking must be done with a view toward sending the right message, not reinforcing the wrong image.

At the same time that professional groups express lofty goals, lawyers in practice feel that the legal profession as a career has become less desirable. Lawyers themselves feel that many in their profession have become more money oriented, putting their own fees before their clients' needs. Lawyers also feel that relationships between lawyers have become more adversarial. The 1997 Florida Bar Opinion Survey reported in the July 1997 issue of *The Florida Bar News*, found that 84 percent of lawyers and all the judges surveyed think the public does not have confidence in the existing legal system.

Lawyers are increasingly uncivilized toward their peers and colleagues, and even their own partners. The 1999 Michigan Bar Quality of Life Survey reported 84 percent of lawyers are concerned about the declining civility of the judiciary and the bar. As the atmosphere of incivility increases, the profession is less and less attractive to those bright lawyers who could make a difference. Another lawyer told us why she left litigation:

> *I got so tired of opposing lawyers lying to me. They were so obnoxious, argumentative, and unpleasant. Getting faxes after five o'clock in the afternoon that had to be dealt with over the weekend, refusing to honor agreements. Life is too short.*

Many lawyers who have chosen to leave their jobs are often looking for the "grass to be greener" elsewhere. Instead, they should do a better job of creating a personal vision for their careers. Many lawyers move away from the problem rather than moving toward something better. Once established in their new positions, lawyers often find themselves even more dissatisfied because they have made sacrifices to move but have no greater job satisfaction. For example, many lawyers leave law firms to go in-house, believing they will no longer have to bill hours; they often do this without researching the cultural differences between jobs and seeking the differences. The in-house lawyer often discovers the loss of support of a law firm and the professional camaraderie of working with other lawyers. She may also lose credibility among her peers and clients. In some corporate law departments, an employee—although a lawyer—does not have the same credibility with captive corporate business clients as an outside lawyer who has the perceived approval of other well-established lawyers. Job-hopping lawyers rarely take time to research and understand these issues.

Many firms and lawyers separate for a period of time only to reunite at a later date. While the firm and the lawyer were parted, both lost experience and advancement. Whatever the lawyer learned elsewhere, it often does not add to the old practice, but instead causes problems with culture and reassimilation.

As the "brain drain" continues, there are fewer seasoned lawyers to teach new ones. While the practice is losing its talent, senior lawyers are less likely to invest in junior lawyers if they expect the junior lawyers are likely to leave and perhaps "take" the seniors' clients. A three-year lawyer told us why she left her large firm:

> *My colleagues and I feel we're not getting any training. Senior lawyers don't want to take the time to train us because they think we'll just leave anyway. So it's a vicious circle.*

The "brain drain" undermines law firms, corporate law departments, agencies, and the profession. We were told about why a medium-sized firm in San Francisco closed its doors in early 1999:

> *The firm had been losing people for years. Finally, they just had to close down.*

Lawyers must recognize the "brain drain" and allocate resources to stop it by improving job satisfaction for themselves and their colleagues.

CHAPTER 6

CULTURE AND PERSONAL STYLE

Culture may be the most significant issue facing law practices today. Many practices don't know what their culture is, nor how to blend a lawyer's personal style or lateral hires into the existing culture. Resolving style or culture dissonance may make more of a difference in retention and job satisfaction than any other single issue.

Culture is one of those "soft" concepts that most lawyers cannot define—and therefore, feel free to ignore as unimportant. Yet, culture affects lawyers every day. Most people either misunderstand discussions of organizational "culture" as dealing with diversity, or understand the concept and don't know how it applies to them. One reason for the confusion is that the definition of culture in organizations is evolving. Professor Edgar Schien author of *Organizational Culture and Leadership,* describes it this way:

> *A pattern of basic assumptions—invented, discovered or developed by a given group as it learns to cope with its problems of external adaptation and internal integration—that has worked well enough to be considered valid and, therefore to be taught to new members as the correct way to perceive, think and feel in relation to those problems.*

June G. Smart, Ph.D., advises that the concept of culture is most easily remembered by the acronym "HEALTH":

- **H**abits and history
- **E**xpectations
- **A**ttitudes, assumptions, and perceptions
- **L**anguage
- **T**rust
- **H**umanistic environment

In a law practice, the culture encompasses not only the entire firm, but also subcultures within the firm and the personal style of individual lawyers. The culture of the practice is affected by the way the firm communicates its values, its power structure, and its history. Culture shifts when lawyers come and go. Mergers with other practices can succeed or fail depending on the merged practice's ability to recognize the differences in the culture of the two organizations.

Practices must recognize and change or support the current culture, as well as make decisions based on culture issues. To do so, the practice must first understand what its culture is. Culture involves both the dysfunctional and the functional methods practices have for dealing with lawyers, support staff, and clients. However, every element of culture permeates the very essence of what the practice is, how it wants to be perceived, and whether it will thrive. Many lawyers leave their practices over fundamental dissonance with firmwide or practice group culture. Many new and lateral hires have personal styles that are not compatible with firm culture, causing immediate but unrecognized and ill-defined job dissatisfaction.

Every lawyer brings diversity that affects his interaction with the practice and thus affects culture. For example, women's views of law firms generally differ from those of men. To learn some of these general differences, consider *Presumed Equal: What America's Top Women Lawyers Really Think About Their Firms*, a book published by Harvard Women's Law Association in 1998 surveying twelve hundred women in seventy-seven firms. Authors Suzanne Nossel and Elizabeth Westfall refused to assume that men were a type of "control group" against which women's experiences would be measured as "normal." In the context of culture, there is no "normal." A woman partner told us why she resigned after being allowed to work part-time at her request:

> *Sure they let me work part-time. But they weren't nice to me about it. They make you feel like you're lazy. Who needs it?*

Another lawyer said:

> *My husband is a lawyer, too, and he is just miserable at his firm. He'd like to take more free time with our kids, but it's just not the culture there. Men don't do that.*

Each practice should understand its own culture. What does the practice say about itself? How do the lawyers describe it during marketing and recruiting sessions? How does the practice act and react as an organization? How do the various departments and offices have their own culture separate and apart from the firm's culture? What do people in the organization do? How is what people do identical to or different from what the practice and its lawyers say it is? What gets punished? What gets rewarded? How does the practice communicate by written and spoken word to community, colleagues, employees, and clients? What nonverbal messages are communicated and received by the lawyers? The answers to these questions help to define the firm's culture and explain common problems.

Formal and informal power structures may exist, and perceived power is sometimes more important to understand than actual power. Do the highest-billing lawyers hold the most power? Do the senior lawyers control the firm? Are the members of the executive or administrative committees the power holders? How is power used as it relates to gender, age, and position throughout the firm?

Where has the firm come from? Who were the firm's founders? Who have been the firm's leaders? What changes and milestones have shaped the firm? How have mergers with other firms affected culture? How have lateral hires impacted firm culture? What has historically been important to both the lawyers and their clients? The answers to these questions reveal where the firm's culture is rooted.

What does the firm see as its mission and vision? Does the firm have a written mission and vision statement? One can rarely move in a forward direction without a goal in mind. Attempting to clarify practice goals often reveals areas of significant agreement and disagreement between lawyers that the firm might not otherwise recognize as the root of job dissatisfaction.

A meshing of two cultures into a productive, joint new culture is essential to the success of the new firm that is created every time a single lawyer is added to the practice. As in business, the failure rate for lateral lawyers is high. More than 30 percent of lateral lawyers depart within three years. In business, about half the new hires in top echelons quit or are dismissed within three years.

A major factor in merger failure is an underestimation of the difficulties of merging two different cultures, management styles, and practices. To some extent, all mergers create a "me" versus "them" relationship. Most people find their methods familiar and comfortable. Therefore, they associate them with success. The firm will never gain the expected synergies and economies if the two merged entities do not strive to achieve a combined culture. Investing in management development and integration programs is common in business to achieve a combined culture.

Even if the merger doesn't fail, success can come with a high price tag. If there is a mismatch of cultures, the best people leave first. A mismatch of firm cultures can also result in lower productivity, personal and personnel problems, and an atmosphere of high anxiety, hostility, alienation, and apathy among the lawyers. During this difficult period of change, pay particular attention to the culture differences in the ranks and act quickly to move to a joint, shared culture.

What is your firm's culture? Are you "counselors," "trial lawyers," "a sweat shop," "family friendly"? Are you "traditional," "sophisticated," "innovative," "thrifty"? Does your firm stress quality, quantity, time, or cost? Do you know? As one senior partner of a medium-sized firm said during recruiting season when the firm's offers were being rejected by its desired candidates because the firm wasn't perceived as special:

> *If all the general practice firms are plain vanilla, what are we? Pint-sized vanilla?*

Practices must understand how to effect and communicate positive changes in law firm culture. They should make an initial assessment of firm culture and individuals' strengths and weaknesses. Many organizations have found it helpful to use lawyer needs assessments—as well as culture surveys of the firm, support staff, and clients—to gain understanding and to identify culture integration needs of the firm. The assessments also assist in prioritizing intervention efforts as they relate to short-, mid- and long-term demands and goals.

A culture survey can also be helpful in creating a culture benchmark to assess growth. The assessment and awareness gained by the survey can move the firm toward a common, shared culture. The firm can then make future plans and leadership decisions based on this common, shared vision of the future.

Assessments and surveys cannot have a positive impact on an organization unless the results are communicated. Most firms are capable of facilitating the creation of assessment tools and surveys that are easily administered. "Softer" communication issues, such as lawyer involvement, feedback, and positioning for action are more difficult. Communication issues are most crucial in affecting the strategic changes warranted by survey results.

Other methods that can be used to change culture are rewards, recognition, specific management practices to demonstrate culture, symbolic activities, human resource policies, and policies and processes that affect the way the lawyers perceive and respond to culture.

A senior partner in a large firm that has been growing rapidly in recent years discussed his firm's view of merging cultures:

> *We call it the "no jerk" rule. No matter how much business the guy has or how prominent he is, if he's a jerk, we don't want him. Period. We've learned the hard way that it just causes too many problems for everybody.*

Practices must develop a shared sense of importance in understanding combined cultures, quickly determine a pathway for getting to a shared, new culture, and communicate to all lawyers an awareness of similarities and differences as well as an action plan to deal with change and integration.

Because culture touches the very essence of everything the law firm does, use leaders to teach the unique culture through luncheons, formal training workshops, and outside retreats. Find a way to communicate what a twenty-year lawyer said:

> *I could make more money somewhere else. I stay here because it's my home. I like the culture here.*

Practices must also provide culture training in the orientation programs for new hires. All the "rules of the road" are communicated at that time. Issues of building safety, road maps for how to deal with problems, and common benefits are discussed. This allows the firm to provide a consistent message to all new hires about the guiding forces of the firm.

Practices must understand that in everything the firm does every day, its culture is being received and reinforced. A thorough understanding of culture, and redirection where necessary, makes a good quality of life for lawyers in the firm possible by allowing room for the personal styles of all lawyers.

PART 2

LEARNING AND CHANGE

Solutions are easier to articulate than to implement. Solutions require an ability to change and adapt to the current business environment, a commitment to the concepts, and a willingness to assist and allow lawyers to develop to their full potential.

Well-known Massachusetts Institute of Technology senior lecturer Peter Senge is also a member of the Society of Organizational Learning, a global consortium of researchers and companies examining learning and change. He and his colleagues have published *The Dance of Change: The Challenges to Sustaining Momentum in Learning Organizations* (Doubleday/Currency, March 1999). Senge details the unacknowledged fact that real change in a firm rarely happens from the top down. Instead, significant change usually starts small, with one team, and spreads to other teams. In an interview in *Fast Company*'s May 1999 issue, Senge identified several self-reinforcing factors that help a pilot program take root:

> *People develop a personal stake in it. People see that their colleagues take it seriously, and they want to be part of a network of committed people. . . . It works. There are real business results—so it's worthwhile to become engaged. But the most fundamental reinforcer of a pilot program is hearing people say they've found a better way of working. Most people would rather work with a group of people who trust each other. . . . Most people would rather have fun at work. . . . Personal enthusiasm is the initial energizer of any change process. . . . [People] want to be part of a team that's fun to work with and that produces results they are proud of.*

Senge identifies challenges of change in three critical areas: (1) challenges of initial change, (2) challenges of sustaining momentum, and (3) challenges of systemwide redesign and rethinking.

When we explored the available research and the views of practicing lawyers, we found that the Best Lawyers and Best Practices have come to understand fundamental concepts that define them and the work they do in a way that differs from those who are struggling. On the assumption that we won't find light by studying the dark, we explored the most prominent aspects of happy, successful, and satisfied lawyers and their practices. In Part Two, we share those insights with you, along with the strategies such lawyers and practices follow. We discuss individual and organizational methods of meeting all these challenges in the context of dealing with lawyers, their special views, and their special issues.

CHAPTER 7

BEST PRACTICES: HOW TO ATTRACT, TRAIN, AND RETAIN BEST LAWYERS

Fairly concrete steps can be taken to achieve improvement in retaining the best lawyers in various stages of practice, regardless of the size of the organization.

A focus on lawyer retention and job satisfaction will result in securing client loyalty and increasing the client base, as well as improving the work environment. Our interviews suggest that lawyers stay in their practices for long periods mainly for five reasons:

(1) Job satisfaction (*This is the best firm—I love it here.*)
(2) Culture (*These are my friends. I like the people here. We enjoy practicing together—I can't imagine practicing anywhere else.*)
(3) Hopelessness (*It's no better anywhere else.*)
(4) Inertia (*It takes too much energy to start over.*)
(5) Bondage (*I can't make as much money doing anything else. There's nothing else I'm qualified to do.*)

We submit that only one of these reasons is worth forty years of your life: job satisfaction. And there is only one way to provide job satisfaction for lawyers: become a Best Practice.

Best Practices have several common traits. They are visionary, always trying to improve their client service and work environment. They make improving job satisfaction and lawyer retention a *goal*. They have established trust between management and lawyers. Best Practices communicate well and often with everyone in the organization, to assure that lawyers feel they are not working in an environment with hidden agendas. They are profitable, pursue worthy goals, recognize the value of all lawyers, and create a culture that is supportive and flexible. They recognize that lawyers are excellent problem solvers. When a problem arises, they share the problem with the involved lawyers, solicit suggestions for resolution, gain consensus, and implement suggested solutions promptly. They find ways to provide exciting, challenging work for lawyers and support them in what Tom Peters, management guru to star corporations, calls "WOW! Projects" in his book *The Pursuit of WOW!* They find ways to let lawyers, often described as "a herd of cats," control and manage their own lives within the parameters of a practice.

Legal folklore is replete with stories about firms that don't want to retain lawyers. They treat lawyers like an expendable resource and don't care if the lawyers treat them like an expendable job. Such practices are based on leveraging low rates for commodity work or partner-to-associate ratios that permit large partner incomes only if the practice stays highly leveraged. If your firm is one of these, and you want to retain that practice style, your focus will not be on retention. Instead, your focus should be on what the group has to offer the short-time lawyer.

But if the practice is attempting to build institutional clients and a loyal client base, the only way to do it is with continuity of lawyers. The most successful practices know that clients choose the lawyer and not the firm, because the practice of law is a relationship business. Clients like to work with lawyers they know. This is not to say that clients want incompetent or inexperienced representation; but we know of many, many situations in which a client did not hire the best lawyer for the job because the client wanted a lawyer she knew and trusted.

After making job satisfaction and retention a goal and then publicizing that goal, good practices align their behavior with the goal. They begin by establishing a credible person who is accountable for lawyer retention. Firms that have moved in this direction typically select the recruiting administrator for this role when dealing with junior lawyers. Assuming the recruiting administrator is well respected and competent for the job, junior lawyers will welcome the interest in their professional development.

Keeping senior lawyers who have the ability to attract and retain clients is much more difficult than keeping junior lawyers. Senior lawyers will want to hear that the firm values them from a partner who has built credibility with them. That partner should be given a title consistent with the retention function, such as "Retention Partner," or "Professional Development Partner." His department should have a budget and he should be able to demonstrate, in a tangible way, the amount of money his efforts have saved the firm in attrition costs and generated in client retention. His compensation should be directly tied to his success and might very well exceed the compensation of the firm's highest-paid lawyers. In a smaller firm, the Retention Partner might also have a part-time practice and receive a bonus based on retention successes.

To jump-start the process, hire a consultant to do a climate/attitude survey of individual lawyers, discover their levels of job satisfaction, formulate a retention plan, and make recommendations to the firm for retention efforts. Hiring a consultant encourages candor from lawyers, as well as demonstrates to the practice—in a visible way—that the firm is both serious about this effort and is willing to spend money to implement it. These surveys should be completed anonymously, and a report on the results should be made to the entire firm or practice area.

Emphasize and publicize what the climate survey reveals is *right* with the practice. Lawyers are risk analyzers. They tend to focus on problems. But chances are, the practice is doing a lot of things that its lawyers like. Try reminding lawyers of the good things about the practice, and focus on those while the practice begins to resolve whatever problems are identified.

Implementation efforts on identified problems should begin within days of receipt of the recommendations. Actual progress toward these recommendations must be promptly apparent and publicized.

Next, market to lawyers and prospective lawyers just as you market to clients and prospective clients. Ask lawyers to explain why the practice is a good place to work and use this information in retention efforts. If the practice can provide a positive reason for lawyers to choose it over other alternatives, the practice will be able to pick and choose the lawyers it wants to add to the team. What the practice is currently doing right is also the backbone of its "Mission and Vision." Lawyers know what they want the practice to be and where they want it to go, but that knowledge may not have been reduced to writing, publicized, and implemented.

Best Practices actually provide—and are perceived to provide—lawyers with the following opportunities:

(1) Flexibility and life balance

- This translates into individual control over one's practice. Of course, an institution must have policies and procedures in place to make it run effectively. However, even exceptionally large law firms are still relatively small businesses. Flexibility is not impossible; it's just inconvenient and requires a little bit more effort. Certainly a "cafeteria plan" can be created to suit individual needs on almost every level.

(2) Culture

- Lawyers want a culture that is supportive and encouraging. They want to work with peers and clients they like and respect. They want meaningful work. Not surprisingly, many studies show that teams composed of people with differing styles and backgrounds are more effective and creative problem solvers than teams composed of people who are similar to one another. Everyone agrees that life is too short to work for jerks. Most lawyers are unwilling to put up with disrespect in any form from colleagues or supervisors, regardless of how much "rain" they make or how long they've been with the practice.

(3) Institutionalized marketing plans

- Most lawyers don't like marketing and don't want to do it because they view it as unprofessional salesmanship. Lawyers want to do good work and have good work to do. They don't want to have to cultivate that work themselves. Firms need to help lawyers market their services in ways that inure to the benefit of the firm and the lawyer alike, but keep the clients with the firm.

(4) Opportunity
- Lawyers need to perceive that the practice provides them with opportunities they want and can't get elsewhere.

(5) Compensation
- The practice must have a compensation system that pays lawyers the market rate and has the potential to pay above market rate. The system must allow lawyers individual control over their incomes.

(6) Great clients
- Lawyers join firms for perceived prestige, opportunity, and clients. Junior lawyers want to maximize their options and get good training. Senior lawyers want sophisticated work and profitability. They want name recognition. One problem with marketing a small or medium-size firm is lack of "brand." Having to explain the practice's identity when seeking new work is demoralizing and eventually more trouble than it's worth unless flexibility, compensation, sophisticated work or personal relationships make it worth while.

(7) Relaxed atmosphere
- Lawyers are not interested in working in a rigid environment. Most of the time, they aren't interested in working in a structured corporate environment. Many have told us they believe they work better in jeans and T-shirts. Many, many Fortune 500 corporations have gone to casual dress every day, and that policy applies to corporate counsel as well. Most of us know something about making people feel at ease, even if we are not completely adept at applying that social skill. Clients and lawyers are no different from other people in this regard.

(8) Team spirit
- If a lawyer wants to be a "lone wolf," she won't be in your cooperative environment. Lawyers join organizations to work cooperatively.

(9) Great facilities
- One senior lawyer told us that spending money on great offices would give clients the idea that the firm could afford such lavish surroundings because rates were too high. This is not true. Clients want their lawyers to be successful. Clients want to feel their lawyers are the best for the job. One fairly simple way to convey success is to look successful, a point

every firm should want to convey to lawyers and prospective
lawyers as well.

(10) Competent support staff
   - Lawyers need reliable help. When they find it, the firm must
     provide what's necessary to keep support staff in place.
     Nothing disrupts a lawyer's life more quickly and thoroughly
     than the loss of a secretary or paralegal. If support personnel
     leave the firm because of the firm's intransigence in the face of
     requests by the lawyer to resolve problems, the lawyer will
     resent it and his work will be affected.

(11) Graceful separation
   - Have a good exit strategy—what we call a process for
     separating gracefully (outlined in Chapter 29).

Best Practices have a mission and vision that create a shared goal that
lawyers can support. Providing quality legal services at reasonable cost is not a
Mission or Vision; it is an entry-level ticket to admission. The Mission and
Vision must be something more inspiring, evolutionary, and revolutionary. It
must be written, specific, and measurable. Creating such a Mission and Vision
is not simple, but it galvanizes the team into concerted action and makes the
practice a formidable force, instead of a roof under which solo practitioners ply
their trade and pay rent.

Lawyer development responsibilities within successful practices do not stop
just because an associate becomes a partner. Indeed, many practices have more
partners than associates now, or are about evenly divided between associates
and partners. If lawyer development stops at any time, the organization loses.

No matter how exciting the first years of law practice are, by the fifth year
most lawyers are looking for something more. They want greater challenges
and greater rewards. They do not want to be bored or burned out. Practices
must help lawyers get work and clients that will keep the lawyers challenged
and engaged. This, of course, means greater challenge to the practice as well.
The clearer the practice's vision, the clearer the path to sustaining challenge.

Lawyers just want to have fun, too. We're not suggesting that practices
schedule a "happy hour" every day and take the whole firm out to the local bar
as they do on television (although there was a law firm in Detroit that had a
cocktail cart circulated every Friday night for complimentary drinks; the firm is
still around, but the cocktail cart has gone the way of the dinosaur—liquor liability for the social host being the culprit). Fun for lawyers in their work and
their work environment is totally different. Lawyers want to be challenged.
They want to learn things. They want to help people. They want to make a difference. Lawyers thrive on difficult tasks and complicated problems. But
lawyers also want and need praise and affirmation. They want laughter, light-
heartedness, and camaraderie. They need demonstrated appreciation. A client
who thinks paying the bill is thanks enough is not a client many lawyers will
keep for the long run.

Best Practices adopt and adapt strategies and tactics that will support the
individual lawyers they want to attract, train, and retain. "Strategies" are broad

outlines of the path one intends to follow. For example, to adopt a more flexible workplace, a strategy might be to allow lawyers to work in complete personal freedom. "Tactics" are the "who, what, when, and how" one plans to get this task done. To achieve a flexible workplace, tactics might include buying every lawyer a laptop computer with modem capability and a cell phone, so that lawyers could access the office at all times and from all locations. "Obstacles" are the issues that might prevent the practice from getting where it wants to go, and "support" refers to the resources the practice has at its disposal or within its grasp to help achieve tactics. For example, if the practice does not have the capital to purchase laptops and cell phones for all lawyers, that would be an obstacle to the tactic for implementing the flexibility strategy. Support might be the option of leasing the equipment, eliminating the need for a large capital outlay on depreciating technology.

Every level of Best Practice Design can be achieved through (1) setting appropriate goals, (2) identifying strategies, tactics, obstacles, and support, and (3) implementing the plan. Examples and explanations are contained in the remaining chapters within Part Two.

CHAPTER 8

BEST LAWYERS: CAREER DESIGN AND CAREER BUILDING

To improve personal job satisfaction, lawyers must be vigilant in taking charge of personal career development at every stage of practice.

Research for this book has included interviews of lawyers with varying expertise. We have talked with judges, government lawyers, law firm partners, house counsel, associates, law students, pre-law students, lawyers working with the "Big 5" accounting firms, consultants, and lawyers who have left the profession to work in other areas. Speaking regularly with lawyers involved in all aspects of the practice has given us a great deal of insight on a variety of issues related to job satisfaction. We have become convinced that the most satisfied lawyers are the "A players"—the lawyers who are "high value added/hard to replace" lawyers. They have control over their lives. They feel their work is meaningful and fulfilling. They live in a balanced environment. These lawyers have good relationships with their clients that include mutual respect. Intellectual challenge is present in the right quantities. They think of themselves as more than billing units. They have become good students of what brings out their personal job satisfaction, when they feel they've done a good job, and what engages their attention and their efforts. They know when they like the work and what they like about it. They consciously choose to put more of whatever it is that they like in their daily work, and to eliminate to the extent possible the things they don't like. They focus on the artistry of what they do. As one successful senior trial lawyer told us, *"I enjoyed this trial so much, I wrote a poem about it."* Best Lawyers figure out what it is about their work that they would do even if they didn't get paid for it, and then they try to limit their work to those things.

The following are common characteristics of the Best Lawyers with whom we've worked and had the good fortune to know:

- Experts in their chosen field of practice
- As busy as they want to be
- Exceptional economic success
- Easy to deal with
- Enjoy good relationships with clients and colleagues
- Epitomize professionalism
- Have a variety and high quality of experience
- Personally happy and satisfied
- Generally involved in long-term relationships in work and in life

Best Lawyers engage in regular career building, designed to find satisfaction in the practice and avoid the struggle that in other lawyers often lasts for years and results in resignation—to the futility of the struggle or from the profession all together. These lawyers design a career they want by developing a career plan that meets their individual needs and makes them successful in their existing environment.

To create an effective "career design," selecting appropriate goals is essential. Excelling is easier when skills are well matched to interests. The challenge is to define one's own optimum career path and devise simple-to-implement methods to get there. Anything that's too hard to do for a sustained period of time will eventually lead to stress, frustration, and abandonment of the goal or the work.

We recommend a five-step process that begins with defining one's mission in work and in life. The second step is to visualize—as a "heart-stopping" goal—one's perfect law practice. After defining what one really wants, the third step is to devise long-term and short-term goals for achieving the perfect practice as one has defined it. Step four is to devise short-term strategies and tactics to achieve the plan, identifying obstacles and support for getting there. The fifth step is evaluation and celebration.

One should understand that a legal career is a twenty-year to forty-year plan and it is the process, or the journey, that is the ultimate goal. What we're suggesting is that one should concentrate more on the means and less on the end, because it is the daily activity that provides the opportunity for job satisfaction. Pace and timing are important, as are patience, celebration, and relaxation. A part of the overall plan should be time to enjoy life. Americans generally love instant gratification. We want everything from fast food to interactive video games with immediate feedback. Based on the flow model discussed in Chapter 10, immediate feedback is important to optimal experience. But daily feedback on appropriate goals will lend each day of practice an aura of job satisfaction that cannot be achieved by focusing daily on long-term desires.

Our work in career building has taught us that "Happy Lawyer" is not an oxymoron. A well-defined process, coupled with gifted insight, helps lawyers to become "A players"—high value added/hard to replace. We've adapted this process from several sources listed in our bibliography, including Laurie Beth

Jones's book, *The Path*; any lawyer can use the process to improve job satisfaction and achieve his vocation by continuing to be a lawyer. The steps below explain how we do it.

STEP ONE: DISCOVERING YOUR MISSION

There are many books available with different methods for drafting personal mission statements. Two that we especially like are listed in our bibliography. Many seminars, software, and other programs that last hours to days are also available. As with most endeavors, discovering your mission is not a "one size fits all" process. A certain amount of self-knowledge is also required. Many career plans are abandoned at the outset by those who try to define their mission and never seem to get it quite right, or because the task is viewed as daunting, time consuming, and difficult.

The process we use follows our axiom that "the easy way is always best." We suggest that you spend not more than two hours on this process and then, once the mission is drafted, live with it awhile and see how it fits. It may need some fine-tuning as you change or life events change, but we often find that the process works well when it is based on intuitive, right-brain thinking rather than the usual, lawyerly, left-brain approach.

In formulating your mission statement, there are a few things to keep in mind. A mission statement is a purpose and direction for your life. It is written, and should be both evolutionary and revolutionary. Your mission is always bigger than your current role. It shouldn't be something for which you've "settled," but rather something that energizes and engages you. Writing a mission statement you can "grow into" is a three-part process:

- Part One: Every mission requires action and action means verbs. Choose your three most meaningful and exciting verbs.
- Part Two: What do you stand for? To what principle, cause, value, or purpose would you be willing to devote your life?
- Part Three: Whom are you here to help? The more specific you can be, the more focused and powerful will be your energy. Pick only one group or cause you most would like to help or affect in a positive way if you can.

Your mission statement will then be Part One + Part Two + Part Three. Revise the language until you like the way it reads, and then leave it alone. Use the forms in Appendix B to assist you in this process.

STEP TWO: VISION MAPPING YOUR PERFECT PRACTICE

Vision mapping is one of the most enjoyable aspects of career design. Again, there are countless resource and research materials to support the concept that visualizing is an effective way to create or achieve desires. Visualization is now used regularly by Olympic athletes, for example. We make no effort to convince you that the technique works beyond suggesting that you try it. It is one of those things that is fun in the process as well as in the result, and worth doing for that reason alone. A vision statement is the end result of what you will have done—your ideal life. The moment you realize you are unhappy or frustrated with a situation is your power point, because now you have a clear picture of how you *don't* want things to be. Imagine the exact opposite of the frustrating situation, and there you have the makings of your vision. Focus on the life you want.

The key elements of a compelling vision statement are these:

- It is written.
- It is written in present tense, as if it has already been accomplished.
- It covers several activities and time frames.
- It is filled with descriptive details that make it real for you.

Use the forms in Appendix C to help you write your vision statement.

STEP THREE: SETTING APPROPRIATE LONG-TERM AND SHORT-TERM GOALS

Long-Term Goals

Long-term goals should be at least five years ahead of where you are now. We prefer a ten-year plan or longer, because we suggest that you need to formulate a lifelong dream that, at least today, is exciting, evolutionary, revolutionary, fun, and worth moving toward. We're looking for something that makes your heart stop—something that, if John Beresford Tipton from the old *The Million-aire* television series came to your door and offered it to you tomorrow, would literally make you faint. Now, wouldn't you think it was worth getting out of bed every day for that?

We recommend you choose a long-term goal that is a real stretch for you—one that, at the moment, you don't see any way in the world you could have. The only "reality check" here is physical limitation. For example, a fifty-year-old woman should not choose to be an Olympic gold medalist in swimming. Otherwise, imagine with abandon!! Use the questions in Appendix D to assist you with formulating your long-term goals.

Short-Term Goals

Short-term goals should be in six-month increments and should count backward from the long-term goal. As if preparing for a trial when you first receive a case, look at the long-term goal as if it is here today, and work backward from there. For example, if your long-term goal is to be a Supreme Court Justice, then immediately before receiving such an appointment, you would have to be nominated. Before being nominated, you could be a law professor, a federal appeals judge, a president, and so on, backward until today. Use the questions in Appendix D to help you formulate your short-term goals.

STEP FOUR: DEVISE STRATEGIES AND TACTICS; IDENTIFY OBSTACLES AND SUPPORT

This is the heart of the daily opportunity to create optimal experience as a lawyer. What we decide to do every day is what makes us excited and satisfied about work, or stressed, burned out, and bored. The important thing to remember is that our satisfaction is completely within our control and depends less on what we do than on *how we structure* what we do.

"Strategies" are broad outlines of the path we intend to follow. For example, to prepare a case for trial, a strategy might be to obtain information in discovery sufficient to support a motion for summary judgment. "Tactics" are the "who, what, when, and how" we plan to get this task done. "Obstacles" are the issues that might prevent us from getting where we want to go, and "support" refers to the resources we have at our disposal or within our grasp to help us achieve our tactics.

To work within the flow model explained in Chapter 10, you are trying to make the daily practice of law more like a game; have concrete and specific goals every day, focus on the task at hand, and devise tasks that provide immediate feedback and fit within your overall short-term and long-term goals. Use the questions in Appendix D to help you with your strategies and tactics.

STEP FIVE: EVALUATION AND CELEBRATION

This is the stage for evaluating results of today's efforts and celebrating success. Many of our career design clients will struggle toward a goal, achieve it, and never celebrate the final outcome or the smaller victories along the way. If you think about this in the context of a game, it helps to recall passing "Go" and getting $200 in Monopoly®; winning the game, set, and match in tennis; winning the hole, the longest drive, closest to the pin, and the round in golf; the first down in football; and so on. The concept is the same. Each stage of the process should have a measurable end that you can evaluate at the time it's finished, and celebrate the victory or adjust performance for the next chance to win.

Setting goals such as "I want to win this case" when the case is first assigned is a long-term goal. A better goal is "I want to win this case on summary judgment." A good strategy is to try to get admissions from the opposing side that will successfully support the motion. Good tactics are to submit requests for admissions or requests to produce authentic documents that contain admissible evidence, or to submit carefully worded questions on deposition. When the requests for admissions are answered and they don't contain the admissions you were seeking, evaluate the reasons and resubmit them. When the "correct" answers come, then celebrate!

Tactics should be further broken down into daily tasks that can be immediately evaluated and celebrated. Each task should be measurable and easily defined, and should present challenges commensurate with skills and desires for the day. Recall that tasks that are too difficult due to time pressures, skill levels, or other obstacles will produce stress and be unpleasant. Tasks should be matched to resources and desires for today's activities.

Celebration is the best part of the process. Of course, to be meaningful, celebration should match the level of success to the task at hand. There are any number of celebrations that are appropriate for the end-of-a-day of success in relatively "small" tasks. Some people give themselves gold stars, or points that accumulate and can be "spent" on a larger celebration. Bigger celebrations might be a weekend away at the beach, an afternoon at the spa, a small gift you may have been wanting for a while, or dinner with a friend you haven't seen. Achievement of long-term goals might call for a party, a bottle of champagne, or a big gift you've been denying yourself.

CAREER DESIGN: A WORTHWHILE INVESTMENT

Career design and career building are every lawyer's personal responsibility. In American society, goals are set for lawyers at every step of the process of becoming a senior lawyer, either as a partner in a law firm or high-level management in a department or agency. Once they achieve the "brass ring," lawyers are often left without guiding goals. Because partnership in law firms comes at about the five-year to seven-year level, and many senior department or agency positions are achieved at the seven-year to ten-year level, that leaves twenty to thirty years of your legal career to design. Understanding that the goal setting that comes after one grabs the brass ring is much more significant and important than the goal setting that comes before is one secret to a lifetime of job satisfaction as a lawyer. Designing a career you can enjoy for the long term is time well spent.

CHAPTER 9

LAWYER ENGAGEMENT

Surveys have found that to increase retention, workers in any type of enterprise must be emotionally "engaged" with the business. The major issues here are trust in leadership and a stake in the outcome. Lawyers will stay with a group if they trust its leaders and if they feel there's a common goal.

Lawyers leave their firms either because they have never become emotionally engaged or affiliated with the organization, or because they've become disengaged. That is, they do not feel a part of the organization and do not have an emotional stake in it. At the junior associate level, a program designed to encourage engagement must begin immediately. In successful practices, junior associates are made part of a practice group, assigned a good mentor, and given a role in firm or practice group management. Within the first six months, every partner in the practice group has lunch with the new associate at least once, and preferably more. New associates are included in informal practice discussions regularly. No new associate is ever allowed to form the belief that the firm doesn't care about him. Thus begins the process of lawyer engagement, essential because engaged lawyers are loyal and committed lawyers.

A midlevel partner in a firm that is self-described as "half litigation, half transactional" and that has about sixty-five lawyers told us:

> The firm's retention in the last two years is going well. The firm is profitable and we have a good group of people whom we take good care of. There's a sense that people want to practice together. We've had nobody leave.

For years, we have suggested that firms should make all lawyers partners. The joke was that "then we can pay them less." In reality, though, several large law firms have understood that making all lawyers partners on some level is exactly what is required. These firms have placed even junior lawyers on committees responsible for significant decision making, including decisions on whether associates are offered partnership. All lawyers must be partners in making the firm a success and they must have a personal reason to do so. Law firms are often like shopping malls; A group of individual lawyers and profit centers operate under one combined roof, but don't act as a team working on the same goals. This multiple-enterprise approach makes a portable practice that can be easily moved from one location to the next as the lawyer matures. The decline of institutional goal setting and institutional clients also contributes to portability. A lawyer who recently returned to private practice after several years of work with the Dalkon Shield Trust told us:

> *I miss the responsibility of decision making and working on a common goal. At the Trust, our goal was to get the cases resolved. In private practice, resolving all the cases usually isn't the goal and there's no other stated goal to pursue.*

Employee stock-ownership programs have become increasingly popular in the business world because they provide a relatively simple and effective way to create a feeling of solidarity with the enterprise and a common goal. Stock-ownership programs give employees an interest in the firm's economic success, improving attendance and product quality and reducing turnover. Productivity, profitability, and stock prices rise after employee ownership programs are adopted. Successful practices find similar mechanisms for encouraging solidarity in associates or nonequity partners.

Given the poor retention rate of law firm partners, one must conclude that economic ownership alone is not an adequate incentive for lawyers to remain engaged with the practice. Many studies reflect that money is a hedge against unhappiness, but money doesn't make Americans happy. Even so, partners do leave less frequently than associates and staff lawyers, so ownership does improve engagement and retention. Recognize, however, that ownership isn't the only issue.

The second element important to lawyer engagement is trust in leadership. Put simply, this means lawyers must believe their leaders and share a common goal beyond mere profitability. Trust is essential for all aspects of engagement; if management isn't trusted by the lawyers in the enterprise, management will be replaced—either by the practice or when the lawyer leaves for a new job.

If the essence of engagement is having an emotional stake in the enterprise, then one of the most effective ways to engage lawyers is to mentor them. A close, personal apprentice relationship can keep a lawyer engaged, or encourage him to leave when his mentor does. A senior lawyer recalled the importance of a mentor's support:

> *On the day of the partnership vote, I was pretty apprehensive about it. My mentor told me if I wasn't voted in, he would resign. I think he would have, too, but neither of us ever had to find out. His support meant everything to me. It's not a coincidence that neither one of us is with that firm anymore.*

Mentees rarely leave their mentors without some encouragement to do so. Developing mentor relationships, and encouraging the mentor to stay with the practice, results in more effective retention.

Lawyers are independent "Lone Rangers." We're trained that way. In the best professional sense, we are accustomed to being in control of a matter, giving advice to the client, and having the client listen and then act according to our direction. As legal careers progress, lawyers develop a client base, which provides more independence. Remaining *inter*dependent in an association of lawyers is a choice that must be encouraged.

"Managing the talent," as they say in sports circles, is not an easy job. "Team building" is the current euphemism for it in business management circles, and the business world has devoted a great deal of research, time, and training to it. The idea has been adopted by the most successful practices.

Edward L. Gubman's book, *The Talent Solution* (McGraw Hill 1998), is subtitled *Aligning Strategy and People to Achieve Extraordinary Results*. Gubman is a Ph.D. global leader for Hewitt Associates' Organization Effectiveness consulting practice. Hewitt Associates LLC is a global management consulting firm specializing in human resource solutions. It serves 75 percent of the Fortune 500, and has seventy-five hundred associates located in seventy offices in thirty countries around the world. Based on that vast experience, Gubman argues that there exists an escalating talent crisis in business today. He reports that companies are finding it harder to fill positions and keep good talent. His book states the proposition that the balance of power in the working world is shifting from employer to employee.

In short, Gubman's hypothesis is that if your enterprise is not "a great place to work," you'll soon find that no one works there. Because Gubman's talent solution deals with managing people, it is not easy to implement, even assuming one is managing "regular people" and not lawyers. Working with lawyers to maximize their individual strengths is much more effective than attempting to change them to fit a mold with which they don't agree.

Gubman's view is that getting your talent engaged with your enterprise is "much more about creating an environment in which people feel energized to do the best work of their careers." (Gubman at 205) Gubman identifies seven factors in employee engagement (Table 11–1) that, we submit, are not so different for lawyers:

(1) Shared values/sense of purpose
(2) Quality of work life (meaning satisfaction with the work environment)
(3) Job tasks that are challenging and interesting
(4) Relationships with managers, coworkers, and customers
(5) Total compensation, including pay, benefits, and financial recognition
(6) Opportunities for growth in learning, additional responsibility, and advancement
(7) Leadership, defined as trust in—and credibility of—the organization's leaders

A large-firm associate, who was a lateral hire and had been with the firm for two years told us this:

> *I want to be an advocate. I love practicing at my large firm because the firm encourages and supports me and gives me credit for my outside activities. I work with people I like. I have the resources to do good legal work. I am very happy.*

Interestingly, a study of British civil servants from 1985 to 1993 showed that a feeling of little or no control at work is the biggest risk factor in heart disease. Other risk factors, such as smoking, inactivity, or high blood pressure are all less important in the development of heart disease than feeling out of control. The research suggests that a rigid organization is the culprit in fostering feelings of little personal control. The more structure involved in the organization, the less likely the lawyers who work there will feel in control of their lives and therefore engaged with the practice. Not surprisingly, lack of control is one main issue that lawyers cite when explaining their dissatisfaction with current jobs. A managing partner told us:

> *I have a lot of control over my work now. Although there are many things I can't control, I have much more information and more opportunities to direct things.*

Lawyers should be asked how they view the quality of work life in their practice and they must be encouraged to give candid answers. Job tasks that are challenging and interesting are easy to create for an entry or midlevel lawyer and many practices take the responsibility to do so. Practices can take responsibility for assuring that challenging and interesting job tasks exist for more senior lawyers, although some practices view acquiring challenging work as a task for the lawyers themselves, with the full assistance and support of their practices.

Management should understand the relationships between coworkers and resolve issues that arise promptly. After all, relationships with clients are addressed in a proactive way. Clients are asked, "How are we doing? What can we do better?" Total compensation including pay, benefits, and financial recognition is given more attention than any other single factor in most American organizations, and law firms are no exception. But managing compensation to improve lawyer job satisfaction by focusing on opportunities for growth in learning, additional responsibility, and advancement—as well as current performance—is a better answer.

Leadership, defined as trust in—and the credibility of—the organization's leaders, cannot be ignored. In law firms particularly, leadership positions are often given to lawyers with the most business or lawyers who are willing to take on the onerous role. In corporations and agencies, leadership positions in law departments are frequently decided by the nonlegal senior management team in ways that sometimes seem mysterious to everyone else. Once a leader has the position in a corporation or agency, she is apt to keep it until she is promoted or leaves the organization. Actual performance as a leader of lawyers is assessed in Best Practices, where leaders are elected or appointed based on demonstrated leadership ability. The leader role must be a prestigious one that lawyers want to perform, not just a job no one wants, which results in ineffective lawyers being placed in the role.

Lawyer engagement is an issue that has received little attention in many law practices partly because practices have not understood its importance to the firm's continued viability and progress. Because many lawyers believe there is a glut of good legal talent, the assumption has been that there would always be another "golden goose" to lay the golden eggs if the current one should leave for any reason. As law school applications decline and lawyers leave the profession, either through retirement or attrition, organizations of lawyers will increasingly recognize they are in the same position as the rest of American business today: facing an escalating talent crisis. Marketing experts tell us that we are five times more likely to get new business from an existing client than we are to get new business from a client who doesn't know us and has not used our services before. Applying the same rules to lawyers, you are five times more likely to keep the lawyers you have than to be successful with the new ones you hire to replace them. It behooves every practice to understand and foster lawyer engagement. Ask lawyers at all levels of the practice why they stay with the firm and then publicize those reasons within the firm and to the firm's clients. Some of the practice's best recruiting and retention tactics will emerge.

BEST PRACTICE STRATEGIES

- Adopt a "we care" attitude about your lawyers and encourage them to become emotionally attached to the firm as soon as they join the practice, and daily thereafter.

- Select leaders who can truly lead your organization. They should be credible and trustworthy, have demonstrated leadership ability, and be capable of inspiring others to greatness. Once selected, leaders should have intensive management training on a regular basis.

- Develop a strategic plan to work toward so that your organization shares a common goal beyond vague notions of "improved profitability."

- Give all lawyers not just responsibility and accountability, but an exciting, inspiring mission to fulfill. Give them a stake in the outcome of firm projects. Joy beats duty every time.

BEST LAWYER STRATEGIES

- Take charge of your career. Make an effort to get involved. Get to know people. Volunteer for committee assignments. Develop an emotional stake in your practice.

- Help lawyers junior to you develop an emotional stake in your practice. Make an effort to enhance their careers. Talk to them regularly. You'll learn something, create a more loyal lawyer, and improve your own job satisfaction as well.

- Look for exciting work and ask your practice to help you get it.
- Work with people you respect and trust. Be sure the people with whom you work can respect and trust you. Credibility is your most essential asset.

CHAPTER 10

FLOW: OPTIMAL EXPERIENCE FOR LAWYERS

Take responsibility for personal happiness. Set clear goals, develop skills, become sensitive to feedback, know how to concentrate, and get involved. Have an overall context within which to live. Job satisfaction for lawyers is primarily related to making satisfaction a goal, and successfully addressing the five elements of time, money, personal style, conflict, and professionalism.

The continued achievement of worthy goals is one definition of success. In that context, life as a lawyer may present one with the greatest potential for success of any job on Earth. Certainly it has the potential to be more flexible, more personally satisfying, and more financially rewarding than many other careers.

Yet surveys repeatedly reflect the low level of job satisfaction and high voluntary turnover among lawyers. Indeed, in *Keeping the Keepers*, the National Association for Law Placement Foundation reported in 1998 that more than 80 percent of lawyers leave their first law jobs after eight years. The 1997 Florida Bar Opinion Survey reported that 70 percent of lawyers are at least "somewhat dissatisfied" with their practices. The 1999 Michigan Bar Survey reported 49 percent of lawyers are dissatisfied.

Psychologists have studied human happiness for decades and have determined the common characteristics of humans in the midst of optimal experience. The basic formula set forth in *Flow: The Psychology of Optimal Experience,* by Mihaly Csikszentmihalyi, Ph.D., is to learn to set appropriate challenges that are neither too simple (which produces boredom) nor too difficult (which produces stress), consistent with one's overall values and upon which one can concentrate fully. In short, to the extent that life is more like a challenging game, the more satisfied one is during and after the process. And the surest way to unhappiness is to measure success in terms of the end result. If one takes a job merely to make money, psychological research shows job satisfaction will be de minimis.

Our question was: How can individual lawyers improve satisfaction with their current jobs, and how can law firms keep good lawyers with the practice? Based on our interviews, reported surveys, and information gathered by psychologists and sociologists, job satisfaction for individual lawyers is primarily about making a commitment to the goal of achieving satisfaction at work and using the flow model to achieve it. Lawyer retention in organizations is primarily about assisting lawyers in their quest for job satisfaction.

Lawyers are looking for exactly what a successful senior lawyer just coming off a month-long trial resulting in a multimillion dollar jury verdict told us:

> *I would do this every day, even if I didn't get paid for it, if I could be in trial every day. I've been really lucky. I do about two trials a year. I look at it like playing golf. I'd play golf every day, too, if I could. I like trying to get better at the game, learning the course, improving my score.*

By contrast, many report experiences similar to those of another we interviewed, a municipal bond lawyer from Virginia turned career novelist who left her practice after five years. She told us why she quit:

> *Why would anyone want to practice law? The work is boring, repetitive, and all consuming. I tried litigation and that was even worse. I looked at the partner I worked for who had been doing this for twenty years and he still worked every Saturday. I didn't want my life to be like that. So I quit my job, started teaching college to make money, and wrote novels. My first year as a novelist I was making $25,000 teaching and $75,000 writing. It's been better every year since then. I can work when and where I want, and I have a lot of personal freedom and more money. This life is a lot better than practicing law.*

No one comes out of the womb knowing how to be a successful lawyer. Learning is required, which is one reason we call it "practice." An element of ongoing job satisfaction is matching skills and challenges during the learning. As an example, asking a first-year, first-day lawyer to try a two-witness, red-light/green-light case two weeks hence would require skills far beyond his expertise. Such a disproportionate challenge to his level of ability produces more stress than anticipation or excitement. On the other hand, an experienced ten-year trial lawyer would find the task boring.

Lawyering is a learned skill and successful lawyering takes years of practice. Often, just as lawyers learn their craft, they leave their practices due to job dissatisfaction, frequently because the job is no longer challenging, intrinsic rewards are not there, and it's no longer fun. Not surprisingly, fun is important. Studies show that when humans are in a good mood, they learn better, solve problems faster, and are more creative. In short, when we *play* at what we do, we do it better than when we *work* at it.

A south Florida real estate partner nearing the age for "early retirement" told us:

> *I had my associate out on maternity leave for a while and I had to draft my own documents. I just hated it. I haven't drafted documents in years and I couldn't wait for her to get back so I didn't have to do it anymore.*

A twenty-year litigation partner in a national firm echoed these thoughts when, speaking of some of the most sophisticated litigation available in the country today, she told us:

> *I am so tired of this repetitive work. I'll be glad when this work is over and I don't have to make these same arguments again.*

Solving the problem of job dissatisfaction among lawyers has been viewed by some as insurmountable because lawyers are often considered to be people who don't want to be happy, and law firm management is viewed as uncaring about job satisfaction for lawyers, support staff, or anyone else. As one lawyer put it:

> *Law firms are terrible places to work. I hate the backbiting among partners. A partner I referred some work to—work that paid his firm over a million dollars—did nothing but try to undercut me with the client. I've had several pieces of business I could have sent to him since then, but I'll never use him again.*

A lateral hire in a medium-sized firm told a similar story:

> *I'm a corporate lawyer and I brought in a big piece of litigation last year. I'm sure the fee on that case was easily the largest single fee the litigators made last year. Yet, it was almost as if they resented the fact that I brought it in, and I'm sure I won't get any fee credit for it. For some reason, the work I'm able to generate isn't in my area, but it's like the firm doesn't want it if I can't do it myself.*

We know that a one-time, easy solution is neither possible nor desirable. If such a solution were available, it would have already been implemented, not only for lawyers but for humans everywhere. But we also know that all challenges can be met. What we can do is to provide individuals and firms with strategies that will improve individual job satisfaction and the quality of work life, as well as reduce voluntary turnover, the same way you eat an elephant: one bite at a time.

The most satisfied lawyers do work that is intrinsically rewarding. A partner in a medium-sized, full-service firm came to the practice of law after several years in journalism. She made the switch because she thought law practice would be "fun." She's happy with the change:

> *It's better than journalism, more intellectually challenging, and it pays better. I was always interested in becoming a lawyer. I covered the courts as a journalist. I thought the law would be fun. I like dealing with people. The days*

I'm with the clients are days that are fun. I like the law. Days are fun when I read cases and write a good argument. I've done something good. Something I'm proud of.

Interviews with lawyers reflect that job satisfaction is primarily a function of a *decision* to be satisfied, and the degree of *control* a lawyer perceives she has over her professional and personal life. If the *perception* of *control* is the overriding objective, job satisfaction is based on how well individual lawyers and firms set and achieve challenging goals that are commensurate with skills, in five broad categories:

(1) *Time:* This includes the idea of a life outside law practice as well as managing one's time within one's practice area. It includes scheduling techniques that help with time management. Everyone on earth has twenty-four hours in the day. Time is the one element that is not expandable. Within that twenty-four hours must fit all of one's personal and professional desires. Proven methods for balancing the competing demands of personal life, family life, and professional life are essential for job satisfaction. Time also affects the other four elements, because successful time management is the fundamental tool that makes the other elements possible.

(2) *Money:* This includes coming to grips with financial needs as individual lawyers and, when lawyers practice cooperatively, as organizations. It includes managing expectations successfully, as well as managing money successfully. The old adage, "It's not what you make, it's what you spend," is half true. A more accurate statement is, "It is what you make, and what you spend, as well as how you spend it." This element includes pricing of legal services, managing the practice with financial goals in mind, marketing, managing expenses, and so on.

(3) *Personal style and culture:* These determine, perhaps more than any other factor, whether a group of lawyers are going to work successfully together. The same is true for working with clients. The aspects of personal style and culture that are important in this context include issues such as (a) whether one is an early bird or a night owl, (b) one's communication style (analytical/amiable/expressive/driver), (c) how one prefers to dress, (d) how one wants to market the practice, and (e) whether one generally plays well with others. More voluntary turnover is caused by differences in personal style and culture than any other single factor. More specifically, turnover is caused by a group of lawyers with one style insisting that all other styles conform to the first group. The more flexible the culture, the more inclusive it will be and the greater the number of lawyers who can live successfully within it.

(4) *Conflict:* This refers to how to deal with the essence of lawyering without having it reduce life to a personal conflict and desire to leave the arena. Conflict is so universally cited as an element of dissatisfaction with lawyering, that it must be independently addressed. Managing conflict effectively is an essential skill for job satisfaction.

(5) *Professionalism:* This includes all aspects of being a lawyer in the highest sense, in the sense of goals and aspirations for the profession, for society and for society's view of lawyers. It includes our desire to be of assistance to

humanity, to do meaningful work, and to make a difference in a larger way than individual representation of specific clients can do. It includes seeking, identifying, and pursuing challenging work at each stage of the practice. Techniques for improving professionalism on an individual and group basis are skills that can be learned.

On a global basis, satisfied lawyers define their vision, discover their mission, and set long-term and short-term goals. They ensure they are pursuing what they want and not merely fleeing what they don't want. The real secret to daily job satisfaction is choosing appropriate strategies and tactics for each goal and devising enjoyable daily tasks for each tactic that meet the flow model. Each daily task must engage one's enthusiasm, be appropriately challenging—but not overly so, and provide immediate feedback. As a legal career develops, choosing challenging goals becomes more difficult and requires more imagination and assistance from the practice. When challenge itself becomes a goal, everyone stays engaged and energized.

BEST PRACTICE STRATEGIES

- Encourage appropriate goal setting by individual lawyers and by the firm. Every lawyer should have a five-year plan that focuses on wishes, regardless of obstacles or support.
- Make sure lawyers have opportunities for challenging and rewarding work. Share intrinsically rewarding firm goals and encourage all lawyers to participate in achieving them.
- Acknowledge goals achieved. Internal newsletters advising the rest of the team when interim goals have been achieved or sharing the progress toward firm initiatives provide necessary feedback.
- Be flexible. Lawyers are high achievers. It is likely that every lawyer in your group has the capacity to be an "A player." Let them demonstrate their talents to the best of their abilities. Don't try to force them into molds that don't fit their personal styles.
- Be supportive. Lawyers want to play by the rules. Lawyers understand rules and understand that the context in which American life is lived is filled with rules. The challenge is to live well within the rules and not to adopt unnecessary ones—they can become a straitjacket.
- Train lawyers to give clients work that the clients themselves value.
- Train lawyers in valuing and capturing time.

BEST LAWYER STRATEGIES

- Develop your vision in law and in life. Do not float aimlessly in your career or in your organization. Determine what you want your life and practice to look like, and then achieve it within the organization in which you find yourself. You have a lot invested where you are. Don't start over. Build on the transition curve by adapting what you know to where you want to go.

- Recognize that setting appropriate goals is the best way to ensure a happy and successful life. Determine your personal and professional goals, and celebrate them when you achieve them. Learn to develop achievable goals that will serve your vision. Goal setting is an art, not a science. Setting goals that are achievable but that slightly exceed your grasp is the objective. Becoming sensitive to the feedback, tweaking your goals as you go along, and staying involved in the process is the solution. Don't accept work that doesn't fit your goals. Wait for work that does. Or better yet, go out and get it.

- Challenge yourself to exceed your perceived capabilities. Adopting challenges and meeting them is the secret to optimal experience. Why do people climb Mount Everest, after all?

- Pursue your passions. If you are anything but passionate about your work, reconsider and revise the kind of law you practice and how you do it. Life is too short (or too long) to toil on work that doesn't excite you. Find something that does. Volunteer for work that interests you. Get on projects that excite you or that you can make into something exciting.

- Become a lifelong learner. Approach every new project with an attitude of excitement in learning something new and different. Enjoy the experience.

- Decide whether you are going to be a specialist or a generalist and stick with it. It's interesting to know that the majority of malpractice claims come from accepting matters in which lawyers spend the least time in their practices. What you don't know can hurt you. Evaluate your interests and the needs of your practice. Market yourself within the practice to fill the needs that interest you.

CHAPTER 11

QUALITY OF LIFE

People first, lawyers second. Although lawyers generally believe they are essential to their clients' lives, much of the joy and the sorrow of law practice centers on lack of balance between personal and professional goals. Happy lawyers feel joy in work, and time to enjoy life is an essential factor. Successful practices address the needs of the whole person in the areas of balance, ownership, renewal, lawyering, and time management.

Life balance is a concept meant to include all aspects of American life: friends/family, romance/adventure, spirituality, work, play, and exercise/health. As Chester Barnard, once president of the New Jersey Bell Telephone Company and later the Rockefeller Foundation, said, "You hire people for their skills, but then the whole person shows up on the job." Selecting law as a career should not mean that lawyers are deprived of the joys of life. Lawyers are people first and lawyers second. They appropriately feel they, too, are entitled to life balance.

Many medium-size to large law firms have some type of policy that allows part-time, flextime, telecommuting, or other alternative work arrangements. The Society for Human Resource Management estimates that a person who works at home two days a week saves the employer $12,000 a year in increased productivity, office space, equipment costs, and turnover. Most practices have maternity, paternity, family leave, and disability policies. One would be hard-pressed to find a major corporation in America that does not have these programs in place. Some firms have sabbatical plans that allow lawyers several weeks of paid time off for personal renewal, after spending a certain number of years at the firm. Yet, lawyers continue to leave their jobs and the profession due to life balance issues. Why haven't these innovative compensation and work programs solved the problem? What can we do to improve the quality of lawyer work life if these programs haven't done it?

One reason that alternative work arrangements have not improved the quality of work life is that lawyers don't use them, either because they don't want to use them or they fear retribution from clients or the practice if they do so. The Florida Bar 1997 Opinion Survey reported that most Florida lawyers took two weeks of vacation, or less, in 1996. Most also reported that they had more than enough work to do. (When we hear that oft-reported comment that there are too many lawyers, we wonder where those lawyers are and why they aren't lessening the workload for the rest of us!)

"Quality of life" as a euphemism for "too much work, too little life" is a common complaint among lawyers. One reason for this is the practice of charging for legal services by the hour. Hourly billing, unheard of a century ago, has made every lawyer a participant in the race against time. Lawyers cope with sleep deprivation, law office economics, biological clocks, and taxes. We see our lives slipping through the hourglass with no room for joy, family, or recreation while we sell our lives in chunks of six minutes each. Like a significant percentage of the American workforce, lawyers are becoming increasingly interested in "downshifting" or "voluntary simplicity," a phenomenon that is gaining momentum. The Merck Family Fund reported that 62 percent of adults agreed with this statement: "I would like to simplify my life." Similar results have been reported by other studies.

A promising junior lawyer told us she was leaving her firm after five years of successful practice:

> *I'm thinking about starting a family soon and I'll want to work nine to five. The lawyers who have children here still work long hours. I just don't see how it would be possible for me to have children and stay here.*

Some lawyers will see that and say it's good she left, because she wasn't "dedicated to the profession" and wouldn't "pull her weight." Perhaps a firm only wants lawyers with "fire in the belly" who will devote their lives to the law. But remember that working nine to five results in 2,080 hours at work each year, more than a traditional "full-time" job. Working husbands and wives now make up about 44 percent of the employed population. Further, the cost of child care generally means that parents must be paid well. A recent survey of seventy-five U.S. cities reflected that leaving one three-year-old for eight hours each weekday in a for-profit day-care center costs between $260 and $718 a month. After-hours and weekend care are substantially more. American business reported that dollars lost to absenteeism, due primarily to family issues, jumped 32 percent between 1997 and 1998; the most frequently cited reason for the increase was demand for more "face time" by employers. Fifty-three percent of Michigan lawyers surveyed reported being concerned about family and child care demands at least once a month.

Americans work more than workers in all the remaining Western countries, and lawyers work more than other Americans. Bruce Bartlett reported in *The Detroit News* on Labor Day 1998 that the average American worked 1,904 hours in 1997, according to the International Labor Office in Geneva, Switzerland. Only the Japanese worked longer than Americans, about 1,990 hours per year on average. Germans worked just 1,573 hours in 1997.

Bartlett also reported that work hours are not only lower in Europe, but they are falling more rapidly than here. Annual work hours have fallen 8.3 percent in Germany during the last ten years, while they have declined just 0.4 percent in the United States. Our Western counterparts also take more vacation— about four to six weeks a year.

Compare that with the typical lawyer. The Altman Weil 1998 Survey of Law Firm Economics reported that median *billable* hours for all firms surveyed was 1,732 for partners and 1,839 for associates; the median ninth decile was 2,213 for partners and 2,234 for associates. (Averages are slightly higher.) We have not found statistics on how many hours lawyers actually work, although an educated guess is that 20 percent or more of the time a lawyer spends at work is not *billable*, making hours actually worked at least 20 percent higher, or a median of 2,078 for partners and 2,206 for associates.

Lawyers tell us there are a number of reasons why they work so much. A fourteen-year lawyer said:

I think it's just my personality. If I didn't do this, I'd probably have to have two jobs just to stay interested.

An eighteen-year lawyer said:

Greed. Pure greed. Everyone wants to make so much money and no one is happy about it.

A six-year lawyer recently diagnosed with a life-threatening illness but still working seven and a half hours a day between chemotherapy, blood transfusions, and hospitalizations, said:

I don't want to let the client down. He's been so good to us. And no one else can do what I do. I'm the only one who knows it.

A ten-year lawyer, explaining why he wasn't attending a practice area seminar this year, said:

I can't really afford the time out of the office. It's a day out there and a day back for a three-day conference. That's a week away. I can't afford it if I want to make partner.

Another ten-year lawyer who attended the same conference didn't see much of it:

I got in very late two nights ago and spent the whole day yesterday on the phone working or working in my room trying to get a brief done. I probably shouldn't have come.

A seventeen-year lawyer told us why she works late into the night:

I don't require much sleep, and I just love the work. I really enjoy it. When there are no people around is the only time I can get my paperwork done.

Thus, client commitments, personality traits, money, advancement requirements, and the joy of working all factor into the lawyer's decision to work long, hard hours for years on end. Lawyers report the problems this workaholism creates in their personal lives and the personal lives of others with whom they

work, but see little hope of changing what they perceive to be the job requirements. A twenty-year lawyer, on his second marriage, told us a few years ago:

> *My first wife left me when my three daughters were very young because I*
> *spent too much time at the office. I was devastated. I didn't see it coming at*
> *all. I missed her and my kids tremendously. I'm determined not to make the*
> *same mistake in my second marriage. I went to my partners and told them*
> *I'm cutting back. They were very supportive.*

Recently, the same lawyer reported:

> *I was the top biller in my firm last year. I got a big new client and we were*
> *just really busy.*

Thus, even with strong motivation, work/life balance requires constant vigilance.

Some firms do have minimum billable hours and other time requirements applied to partners as well as associates. In those circumstances,
lawyers feel pressured to meet such obligations and then resent the pressure.
But often, workaholism is self-induced, and we have yet to meet a satisfied
workaholic.

Many lawyers fear the loss of business and resultant loss of income, so they
take whatever work comes their way, get overcommitted, overworked, and
resentful. Others are competitive with their colleagues, family, and neighbors
for "success." In short, all the reasons people work too much in other careers
apply to lawyers as well.

Whatever the reasons lawyers give for leaving their firms, you can be sure
that seeking to improve "quality of life" is at or near the top of the list. If law
firms and departments don't figure out a way to manage expectations so that
lawyers can practice law and have a life simultaneously, attrition rates will continue to climb.

All change begins with a change in thinking. Life and law can coexist.
Lawyers must recognize that managing one's career is up to the individual, and
practices must fully support the individual lawyer's choices. They must encourage lawyers to take advantage of part-time and flextime work schedules. Allowing lawyers to control their incomes by controlling their workload is also a simple matter. If compensation is tied to performance and revenue production,
not to seniority or comparisons of one lawyer with another, each lawyer can
individualize his or her situation.

Lawyers are trained in the craft of lawyering through apprenticeship, self-
education, and formal continuing education programs in a lifelong learning
process. Other aspects of a lawyer's training, such as time management and
practice ownership, as well as personal and professional renewal, should be
addressed. When lawyers become vaguely dissatisfied, practices should be
aware of the issues and deal with them promptly.

Junior lawyer training should follow a two-track approach: Junior lawyers
should be trained as career lawyers and future co-owners of a business. Often
when a lawyer reaches partnership, his preset goals have all been met. The challenge of forging a twenty-five-year career has just begun and he is ill-equipped
to create and build that career. A seven-year lawyer just elected to full equity

partnership said, *"Now what will I do?"* The most successful practices offer guidance long before this juncture.

Practices should train associates in the joys and perils of ownership roles and management. Associates should be trained in leadership, accounting, marketing, human resource management, billing, and collection. All lawyers could benefit from basic training in the financial realities of the law business. Lawyers often do not understand concepts such as firm overhead and capital investment, although they are somewhat self-evident. This lack of information leads to unrealistic compensation expectations, particularly by junior lawyers.

Lawyers should be trained in the relatively simple economics of time management. Beyond being given minimum billing guidelines, lawyers are shown how to capture all their time, and how to bill it and collect it, as well as how to increase the amount of revenue they themselves are able to generate as hourly billing units. The concept of value billing and its application is addressed. The mere math of the matter is that capturing and recording time so that it gets billed and collected does more to improve profitability than either increasing the number of hours billed or increasing hourly rates.

If, for example, a lawyer bills 2,000 hours at $100 per hour, and 100 percent of his time is reported, billed, and collected, he will generate $200,000 in revenue. This is the method many lawyers and practices use for budgeting and forecasting. Often, these budgets are not met and projected profits are not realized. More typically, if the lawyer works 2,000 hours but reports only 80 percent of his time (that is, 1,600 hours), bills 90 percent of his time, and collects 80 percent, he will generate only $115,200, a shortfall of $84,800. To improve the amount of revenue generated, the most effective measure for the individual lawyer is to capture and report more of the time actually worked. Still, if the lawyer captures and reports 100 percent of his time (that is, 2,000) but only 90 percent is billed and 80 percent collected, he will generate only $144,000, leaving a shortfall of $56,000. If the practice bills and collects just 5 percent more of the time reported, the same lawyer's 2,000 reported hours would return $161,500, reducing the shortfall by $17,500, *without the lawyer working an extra minute.* Conversely, even if the lawyer reports 100 hours more than 2,000 (that is, 2,100) but the billing (90 percent) and collection (80 percent) practice is not improved, revenue will still fall short of projections (that is, $151,200, or a shortfall of $48,800).

Thus, the key to increasing revenue is for lawyers to learn to value their time properly, to capture it in the billing process, and to be sure that 100 percent of recorded time is billed and collected. Profitability is more about increasing revenue than decreasing expenses. Though keeping expenses down is essential, at some point more revenue must be generated. Focusing on the value of the work performed, billing all the time reported, and using effective collection procedures do far more to increase revenue than increasing the hourly reporting requirements for lawyers. Many lawyers echoed a senior litigator in a small practice:

> I wanted to work less and make more money. So I sat down with a pencil and figured out how to do that. I've decreased my time at the office by half and I made more money last year than I ever have—seven figures.

Second-generation time management techniques are needed to schedule a lawyer's time properly. Paperwork and people work are the two main aspects of the job. One leads to the other, and one must put enough time on the schedule to accommodate both. For example, back-to-back depositions will require written deposition reports to the client. Contract negotiations will precede a written contract. Client meetings will generate written assignments. Presentations require preparation. When Best Lawyers schedule their time they give their secretaries directions such as, "Every deposition must be followed by at least an hour in my office for reporting to the client." The secretary never fills the calendar with "people work," thus leaving the paperwork to be done at night, at home, or on weekends. A simple instruction means the difference between an evening with family—and a happier lawyer—and another late night at the office.

Lawyers are problem solvers by nature and training. Yet, they solve problems based on what they know. If practices offer different insights, then lawyers are not left to form conclusions based on myopic, self-absorbed views that are simply not valid. At a recent meeting of the Association of Legal Administrators, very sophisticated law practice managers had several opportunities to address flextime for lawyers and support staff. Despite the fact that lawyers have always spent large amounts of time out of the office on client matters, these administrators had great difficulty accepting that lawyers could work at remote locations and on flexible schedules. Without having tried it, the administrators came up with several perceived logistical problems to confirm their view—and their firms' views—that flextime for lawyers was not possible, despite others in the audience who clearly stated that flextime worked very well in their practices.

Indeed, one successful small firm has been a "cooperative practice." A boutique litigation practice specializing primarily in medical products liability defense. The firm's lawyers, and paralegals all have flexible schedules, work from remote locations, and have complete control over their personal income. The firm is very successful, highly profitable, well respected by its national clients and lawyers throughout the country, and hasn't had a single person leave the practice since it started.

This cooperative practice started because after fifteen years in litigation, its founder needed some personal freedom. She wanted to spend summers at her lake house in another state and to concentrate some time on writing, as well as serving the legal profession through her consulting work. We have become aware of many similar flexible arrangements that serve the needs of lawyers as whole people, not just billing machines. Invariably, senior lawyers leave their practices for more control over their lives. Make it possible for lawyers to control their lives in your practice and they will stay.

BEST PRACTICE STRATEGIES

- Put more fun in the practice. Enjoy the time spent in the office. Make the office a place lawyers want to spend their time.

- Create an atmosphere where rewarded achievement is something more than celebrating the monthly figures on the accounting books.

- Encourage lawyers to enjoy life, and to get involved in activities other than the practice of law for reasons other than the potential to generate business or satisfy pro bono requirements. Adopt policies and encourage lawyers to use them.

- Do not reward lawyers for behaving badly toward others, failing to treat others with respect, or "acting out" under stress. Instead, encourage lawyers to take a break, to take on less work, and to relax more.

- Limit the number of billable hours that will be rewarded. For example, if the practice's minimum billable hour requirement is 2,000, do not pay a bonus, give time off, or otherwise reward hours billed over 2,000. Hours over 2,000 might be carried over to the next year to allow for additional vacation time; require that lawyers take the extra time off.

- Where possible, set fees on a value to the client basis instead of hourly rates. Reward working smarter, not working longer.

- Adopt an "on call" strategy similar to that of physicians, where lawyers trade taking client calls for each other during vacation times. Client "stealing" should be strictly forbidden.

- Consider turning off the fax machine at 5:00, and the phone, too. If your clients cannot accept this concept, perhaps you can share responsibility with other lawyers for fielding faxes and calls after 5:00, so that each of you doesn't have to be available every day to respond. Many businesses provide coverage twenty-four hours a day, seven days a week, but they don't ask the same person to provide that coverage.

- Encourage telecommuting, particularly in areas where long commutes interfere with the quality of life.

- Design performance reviews—for junior and senior lawyers—to reward a balanced life outside the office as well as inside it. Lawyers should be able to do their jobs in the forty-hour workweek except when they are involved in extraordinary efforts such as collective bargaining sessions or real estate closings. Reward those who accomplish their work in forty hours and then nurture their private lives.

BEST LAWYER STRATEGIES

- Take charge of your quality of life. It is your responsibility to make your life what you want it to be. Put your time where your values are.

- Put more fun in your life. Make a deliberate effort to laugh and be light-hearted. Don't take yourself too seriously. Go to a comedy club, see a funny movie, play more, listen to great music, ride a roller coaster, live.

- Make peace with your practice's expectations. Either accept them as for-mulating the quality of life you want, or decide to go your own way and accept the consequences. A billable-hour culture rewards long hours, not efficiency or working smarter. If your practice insists on a billable-hour culture, either make peace with that or move to another type of practice.

- Always have a "Plan B" that allows you an opportunity to do some-thing else if your practice isn't satisfied with the amount of energy you are willing to give it. Knowing you are practicing law because you *choose* to do so makes all the difference in your mental attitude and per-sonal satisfaction level.

- Figure out how much is enough for you—enough work, enough leisure, enough money, enough stimulation, enough of everything. Stop trying to have as much as there is of everything. We live in an abundant country and there will always be more than enough.

- Remember that the parts of your life you don't nurture will whither and die. If you don't attend to them, they are not as important to you as you say they are. There is a psychological cost to failing to meet your own expectations. Change your expectations or change your behavior. If you always do what you've always done, you'll always get what you've always gotten.

- Master time management techniques that you can accept and that give you more personal freedom. Be sure you capture all the time you spend on client matters. Do not overcommit or promise more to clients than you can deliver. Do the most important tasks first. Keep a prioritized list of today's activities in front of you at all times. Return phone calls at a set time every day and don't allow calls to interrupt your work at other times. Delegate appropriately and assign deadlines for complet-ing delegated work. Don't travel for business on weekends. Move away from billing your time by the hour. Choose practice areas where flat fees can easily be charged and where you will be genuinely helping others rather than simply controlling damages or getting your clients out of trouble they created for themselves with their eyes wide open.

- Understand that life balance is possible. Then figure out how to get it for yourself. Those lawyers who live a balanced life do so because they believe they can and they work at it.

CHAPTER 12

PERSONAL RESPONSIBILITY

Responsibility for designing a successful legal career is the lawyer's alone. Career design and career building are the lawyer's best strategies for avoiding boredom and burnout. Understanding the five stages of a legal career will assist lawyers in analyzing their needs. Lawyers must communicate their needs and seek their own individual solutions.

Lawyers have high expectations of themselves and they want to succeed in life, as well as in law practice. At the same time, lawyers have little or no training in goal-setting techniques, career design, or career building. As a lawyer progresses through the stages of law practice, designing and building a great career to ensure job satisfaction and retention increase in importance. Many lawyers leave their jobs because they are presented with "a better opportunity." Not knowing how to turn their current jobs into ones that are more challenging and potentially more rewarding, they accept the predesigned challenges presented by a recruiter or a client offering a new job. Creating more rewarding jobs with their current practices is usually possible and less disruptive to their lives. Career design and career building are ways to do that.

Recognizing that a law practice develops in certain fairly well-defined stages is the first step to designing a career that will be successful for the individual lawyer. A successful, fun, rewarding, and challenging legal career is within the grasp of every lawyer, and can be had without fleeing the practice or a current association. All it takes is a little planning and diligence.

Understanding the stages of a developing law practice is the first step.

(1) Stage I: The introductory lawyer
   - Getting admitted to an accredited law school, passing the bar exam, and finding the first job complete Stage I. This is where career design has its first opportunity to be effective and where

it is rarely considered. Many, many law students take initial jobs where they will not thrive. The early attrition rate among this group (25 percent after two years) is proof. A better way is to begin in law school to determine interests, discover a mission, and prepare the earliest vision of law practice. Lawyers who interview for jobs that fit within their mission and vision—rather than accepting jobs and hoping they will discover what they want to do once they get hired—will stay in their first jobs longer.

(2) Stage II: The early years

- The lawyer is searching for a specialty, paying back debt, developing expertise, and finding his niche. Again, career design and career building often fall by the wayside. Sixty percent of lawyers leave their first jobs at this stage, demonstrating that the levels of job dissatisfaction for the Stage II lawyer result most often in "flight." Instead, use Stage II to move toward your vision. Have clearly defined goals and enjoy the learning experience. Satisfied lawyers are perceived well by their practices and have little apprehension about continued advancement. Because such lawyers are pursuing their own paths, they are satisfied in the jobs they choose.

(3) Stage III: The middle years

- Here, many lawyers have given up the idea of a great career, decided to accept the unsatisfactory nature of legal work, and focus on outside interests for fun and fulfillment. This is the time when many lawyers are getting married, having children, and accumulating material possessions. The life balance issues related to working and parenting, combined with job dissatisfaction, derail many Stage III careers.

- The happiest lawyers reevaluate their goals in Stage III to be sure they are still on track, and make changes when necessary. They understand that their life circumstances and perspectives may change with experience and expertise. They use the goal-setting and vision-mapping tools they've mastered to help them stay satisfied, challenged, and engaged with the practice.

(4) Stage IV: The long-distance runner

- The challenge in Stage IV is to stay interested. Stay fresh. Have fun. At this stage, many lawyers are doing boring work that is below their level of expertise and that does not interest or excite them. They often make substantial sums of money and accumulate significant wealth, but have no greater level of happiness than in earlier stages. This is despite the recent ten-year study completed by the MacArthur Foundation Research Network on Successful Midlife Development, reflecting that in the years between thirty-five and sixty-five (and the decades between forty and sixty years old in particular), the population in general reports greater increased feelings of well-being and control over their lives. The research debunks the "midlife crisis" theory, too: only 23 percent of the eight thousand participants in the study reported any midlife crisis at all.

- Lawyers must understand that stress and "crisis" are mental games over which they have complete control. They must continually challenge themselves and their practices, and commit themselves to lifelong learning and to life outside the law.

(5) Stage V: Retirement and slowing down

- This is the time when lawyers work just to have something to do with the rest of their days, proving once again that law is a vocation.

Each stage has its pitfalls and rewards, its opportunities for excellence, and its challenges. Recognizing each stage and its relationship to the others is the first step to successful career building. Understanding that each lawyer is a solo practitioner with an obligation to find personal and professional satisfaction puts the accountability for success where it belongs: with the individual lawyer.

Best Lawyers practice in a variety of environments and in many different practice areas. They have the luxury of designing their own careers to suit their personal tastes and they contribute more to their organizations. They have control over their time and compensation. They are successful on their own terms. They are in demand by employers, clients, referral sources, and colleagues. They may not know where the next piece of business is coming from, but they are more secure in the knowledge that the business will be there than other lawyers. Lawyers who achieve this enviable level of success do so by traveling a variety of paths; it is not possible to adopt a cookie-cutter "modeling" approach to career design. After unsuccessfully attempting to model such behavior, aspiring lawyers often conclude that the successful lawyer was just lucky.

Best Lawyers and their organizations are lucky, if that means the lawyers made their own luck by taking control of their professional development, designing their own careers, and being prepared to take advantage of the opportunities presented to them. Building a legal career by moving in whatever direction the wind blows is sometimes successful and sometimes not. Lawyers tell us that they specialized in, say, environmental law because in their first law job they were handed a case that led to a case that led to—well, you get the idea. Eventually, those lawyers find some level of success. Or they reach the point where their work is plentiful but lacks challenge and excitement or is otherwise vaguely unsatisfactory. As one eighteen-year lawyer who describes himself as generally happy told us, *"Let's face it—there's not much intrinsic reward in what we do."*

Legal careers are often gifted with opportunities to develop that are not necessarily in a lineal path along a particular plan. Evaluating those opportunities and taking appropriate advantage of them is one mark of the "lucky" Best

Lawyer. Providing and encouraging those opportunities is a characteristic of this group. Many a lawyer has been devastated at the loss of certain big clients or business areas and later found a much more successful practice. Indeed, many unexpected bends in the road are not the end of the road, but the opportunity for bigger and better things, if one is prepared to accept the challenge.

Lawyers who are satisfied with the work in later stages of the practice have reconciled themselves to the challenge of keeping the work fresh. An eighteen-year environmental lawyer told us she would do this work even if she didn't get paid for it:

> *I love what I do. My clients are my friends. I've been representing some of them for seventeen years. They need me. They wouldn't know what to do if I wasn't there for them.*

A twenty-nine-year general practice litigator with a smaller firm told us:

> *I like the work. It's challenging for me. I like to learn new things and to help people. I'll keep doing this as long as people want me to do it.*

A twenty-seven-year medical device litigator with a large firm said:

> *The work has been really good for me. I've always felt challenged. To be involved in this work, at the level I've been involved, has been a great experience. I like the autonomy of it. I've always been pretty much able to handle my cases without interference. I'll be sixty soon and I'm trying to decide what I'll do then. I'm thinking about doing pro bono work.*

The best career design and career building advice comes from another lawyer who doesn't have a hidden agenda. Try to find a mentor with your best interest at heart. Modeling successful career paths of others and career coaching by knowledgeable consultants are also excellent sources of career design assistance. You want a different perspective and some concrete strategies and tactics for advancing your career.

The foundation for building a successful legal career is the *desire* to have a satisfying career. Without that goal, a lawyer will settle for a lot less from the practice and seek happiness from other endeavors. Given the flexibility of the profession, achieving daily job satisfaction is far from illusory. Many, many senior lawyers have enjoyed the practice for their entire working lives. But they don't allow themselves to become bored by doing repetitive work below their skill levels just to make money, nor do they allow themselves to burn out. A sixty-six-year-old insurance defense lawyer said:

> *You have to pace yourself. You can't get everything in the world done today. You have to save some energy for tomorrow.*

Career building generally means marketing one's services, a task at which the most successful lawyers have learned to excel. They view marketing as a part of their practice plan. They set marketing and career-building goals in the same way they set practice goals. Best Lawyers view marketing as nothing more than letting potential clients know the lawyer is ready, willing, and able to work. They begin their marketing efforts in comfortable surroundings, such as by marketing their skills to their practice colleagues or close friends. They set easily achievable daily marketing tasks, such as taking a colleague to lunch to discuss an exchange of business or writing three short notes to existing clients. Small, manageable goals that can be accomplished are far better than a daunting wish list that seems impossible to get off the ground. Try breaking any task into ten or more tiny steps instead of two or three large ones. A feeling of progress will keep you moving forward.

Happy lawyers know they attract business and clients, not acquire them. They realize that clients select lawyers with whom they have developed relationships, and that lawyers never know where their next piece of business will come from; so they make it a point to become involved in activities they enjoy with people who share their interests. The more people one knows, the more likely it is that one will attract business, if you let people know you want the work.

Lawyers must take personal responsibility for creating satisfying practices. They should understand that career design and career building are lifelong processes, and treat them as a part of the fun of lawyering.

BEST LAWYER STRATEGIES

- Recognize and take personal responsibility for designing and building a successful career that includes job satisfaction at every stage of practice.
- Develop expertise and the aura of expertise that will provide you with an exciting, stimulating career for the long term. Then allow your career to develop over the years. Understand that you don't have to have everything right now. You need something to look forward to.
- Become a comfortable marketer of your talents. Recognize that there are two sides to the fulfilling work equation: doing good work and having good work to do. The more self-sufficient you are, the more valuable you are to yourself and to whatever practice with which you affiliate.
- Affiliate with a Best Practice and do your part to make the practice the Best.
- Once you decide on goals, go after what you want directly and with singleness of purpose. Pass up opportunities that will take you in a different direction, unless you want to change direction.

CHAPTER 13

FLEXIBILITY

There is one sure way to keep lawyers and keep them happy: to paraphrase W.C. Fields, "Give the people what they want." It does no good to insist that systems are "fair" or "reasonable" if they are not satisfactory to the lawyers who work with them.

Perceived lack of flexibility is one of the most amazing aspects of job dissatisfaction for lawyers. Time and again, we are told of work relationships severed over fairly simple issues that could have been easily resolved but were not because the firm or the lawyer was inflexible. The most successful lawyers and practices apply creativity to managing their own law practices.

For example, one large firm we interviewed told us about a talented associate who worked part-time. The associate was married to a high-level executive of a corporate client of the firm and, for "corporate spouse" reasons, needed to be free on Fridays. This system worked quite well during the time the lawyer was an associate. She was—and was perceived to be—a valuable member of the firm, both because of her work and because she brought in business well in excess of her own cost to the firm.

When this associate was due to be considered for partnership, instead of considering an economic solution that would have allowed the lawyer to stay at the firm, the firm refused to make her a partner because she still wanted to work only four days a week. The firm had never had a "part-time" partner before and was unwilling to try it. The lawyer left the firm, and her business—including her husband's corporate employer—left with her.

Another example of inflexibility involved an associate with a unique personal background; he had developed an entertainment agent/law practice that was very lucrative. The practice brought in fees in two dimensions: the agency fee when contracts were signed by sports and entertainment figures, and the additional legal business from those clients in real estate, business ventures, and estate planning.

At the associate's review, he was told that he wasn't billing enough hours, despite having generated far more income for the firm than he would have generated by billing the requisite time. The firm told him that its budgeting and compensation systems were based on billable hours and he would have to bill time like everyone else if he expected to remain employed. He left, taking his clients and his client development potential with him to another practice that was more flexible.

Instead of allowing this type of issue to divide them, practices and lawyers can fashion an economic solution that satisfies them both; they must recognize that dedication to outmoded systems without considering their usefulness in today's workplace is self-defeating for the practice and the lawyers who work there, as is fear of potential problems before they ever materialize. When we examine the issues that create inflexibility, we learn that they are often based on unspoken assumptions.

A partner in a boutique firm with large clients and significant cases said:

I won't hire new lawyers anymore. I am unwilling to pay them $100,000 for the amount of work they want to do. If I'm in there working on the client's problem on Saturday, I expect them to be there, too. I want and need that level of commitment. So, I hire lawyers with some experience who are dedicated to the work. I have to pay them a little more, but I get the level of commitment I want.

In other words, she found an economic solution to her "commitment" problem. She hired more senior lawyers who were willing to work more for more money. A similar economic solution is possible in many, many cases.

A human resources partner in a large northeastern firm said:

One of these days at least one large firm is just going to lead the way and say to new hires that we won't pay you the big salaries, but we'll let you have a life. Do you think they'd take the job if we did that? Or should we all just keep telling them we emphasize quality of life when we know we will still demand these incredible hours?

A lawyer-turned-recruiter who worked in private practice for two years in three different jobs before joining a recruiting firm talked about the things she saw in practice, as well as in her work with lawyers looking to relocate:

There seems to be this "fraternity boy" attitude prevalent among senior lawyers. Sort of, "We had to do it, so you have to do it." But it's obvious the whole practice has to be redefined. Firms have to be more flexible.

This lack of flexibility is apparent not just in the retention of lawyers. It is pervasive throughout the management of some firms and keeps them from effectively competing in the marketplace. For example, one lawyer who has worked at a large firm, as in-house counsel, and now with one of the "Big 5" accounting firms, described why his department—which specializes in consulting with law departments of major corporations worldwide—does not often work with law firms:

The process for getting a project approved in most law firms takes way too long and is too hard to do. There's an endless process to go through. From a mar-

*keting perspective, it is just not effective. It comes down to management phi-
losophy. The "Big 5" are very quick. There's a lot of decentralized management
that is very unlike law firms. We have complete discretion and we move
quickly. We know sometimes we're going to be wrong, but we gain the advantage by staying ahead of the curve.*

The perception that law firms are too inflexible and slow is shared by most
service providers. It ensures that law firms stay "below the radar" of experts
who would keep the profession abreast of current trends and encourage
change. This prevents law firms from taking advantage of the expertise that
helps other businesses to grow and thrive in our rapidly changing world. The
only constant is change, and the failure to change ensures extinction. Instead,
seize the opportunities that present themselves to improve the business, retain
lawyers, and keep the practice current.

The 1999 America Work Study surveyed 1,800 workers; among other things,
the study found that employers who help employees with the demands of life
balance are most likely to keep people for the long haul. (Of course, the study
also suggests that the "long haul" these days is six years.) Half the respondents
said they would consider leaving for a 20-percent raise, but not for less, if their
employers focused on life balance, personal and professional growth, customer
friendliness, and easy access to information about employee benefits.

Similar results have been obtained in a number of studies. In 1998, the
Families and Work Institute surveyed 2,877 employees, 63 percent of whom
said they would like to reduce the number of hours they work; in 1992, only
47 percent wanted to do so. Seventy percent of working parents said they did
not have sufficient time with family.

Conversely, these needs are not being met in the workplace and in professions. Catalyst surveyed 2,000 managers and professionals in four companies
in 1997, and found that 11 percent of women and 4 percent of men worked
part-time compared with 21 percent and 8 percent, respectively, of all working
women and men. The continued emphasis on "face time," or the number of
hours spent in the office rather than on the work produced, is one problem in
the implementation of policies most law practices have in place.

Deloitte & Touche, another "Big 5" employer of lawyers, has instituted a
retention program that covers evaluation, promotion, mentoring, and
work/life flexibility. Turnover has decreased as much as 30 percent in some
offices. Flextime, part-time, and career development at the discretion of the
lawyer and other employees are at the heart of Deloitte's flexibility plan. Surprisingly, many law practices continue to resist these initiatives, thinking that
they will decrease client service. Yet, clients are not the first to complain when
a lawyer doesn't work "24/7"—his partners are!

An example of flexible thinking that is counterintuitive is the recent
research that suggests it is good to sleep on the job, particularly in high-stress
professions. A think tank called the Trends Research Institute reports that
encouraging napping on the job—complete with employer-provided pillows
and blankets—is a growing trend as a strategy for dealing with fatigue.
Research now suggests that breaking up the day with a nap increases efficiency
by correcting the loss of alertness that occurs over time, New York University's

Medical Center/Sleep Disorder Center reports. As one employer put it, "Why do only a good job when you can do a great job?" Lawyers typically bill their time by the hour. So, in a very real sense, a thirty-minute nap costs money, at least in the short run. If it improves efficiency and increases alertness, therefore making the work product better with less effort, lawyers need to formulate methods for billing that reward, not penalize, the innovation. Working smarter has not been a top priority for lawyers because working longer produces more revenue. This must change.

Another counterintuitive fact is that an active personal life enhances effectiveness at work. The *Journal of the American Medical Association* reported in 1998 that people who have active lives outside their work are four times less likely to be sick than others. It is also true that the best and most successful rainmakers are those lawyers who are active in making relationships and contacts outside the firm. It doesn't matter what you do—as long as it gives you the opportunity to meet people who might be clients, you are enhancing your chances of getting new business.

Yet, many lawyers tell us that billable hours and firm expectations leave little time for a life outside the law, particularly for lawyers with children. Simple math proves this to be true. If a lawyer is expected to bill eighteen hundred hours a year (which is low for many top-tier firms), and if about 20 percent of the lawyer's time spent in the office is not billable (a very conservative estimate), then a minimum of nine hours at work is required for each twenty-four hour day (assuming a five-day workweek and a forty-eight-week work year), leaving fifteen available hours. Seven hours of sleep each night reduce the available hours to eight. Bathing, grooming, and eating dinner will take a minimum of an hour and a half more (if you're quick, skip breakfast and eat a working lunch), leaving six and a half hours a day for everything else, including commuting to work. Clearly, lawyers are not the "average Americans" who are reported to watch seven hours of television each day. Nor does such a schedule leave time for civic and pro bono activities. A single, four-year lawyer explained why she changed jobs:

> *My prior firm supported my civic and pro bono efforts, but that work was done in addition to the 1,900 billable-hour requisite, and was very separate from my legal work for the firm. I took a pay cut, but the reduction isn't that great when hours are down and I'm happier.*

A six-year lawyer left the practice of law altogether due to what she perceived as the lack of control and lack of flexibility of a law practice after the birth of her daughter:

> *I was very happy practicing law for a very long time. But after my daughter was born, I wanted more control over my life and flexibility in my work schedule. My firm was very supportive and even let me handle my lawyer placement service out of their offices for a time after I stopped practicing. I feel I am much more suited to this than I was to practicing law and it allows me time to be with my family when I think it's important to be there.*

A sixteen-year lawyer in solo practice for thirteen years told us she started her solo practice to improve her level of job satisfaction:

I'm a night person. I love what I do and I really get into it. But I need the people to be gone to focus on the paper. I work until late in the morning and it's hard to get going when I work late. This was unacceptable in private practice. And I hated making excuses when I wanted to go get my hair done or go to the dentist. Now, if I want to, I take a one-month vacation.

A recent two-year study by Purdue University shows that customized work arrangements made 90 percent of the respondents happier with work/life balance and boosted productivity. Flexibility is harder, but not impossible, for large firms that have a need for structure to assure fair treatment to all lawyers. Best Practices implement a cafeteria plan of choices, which can themselves be adjusted.

Flexibility issues are a top priority on the list of many lawyers, firms, organizations, and bar associations today. Burnout and frustration are real problems that cause lawyers to leave their practices and the profession. Resistence to flexibility is often couched in terms of feared future problems, rather than actual issues presented. Management worries in advance about two primary issues: Why should we offer such flexibility? How will flexibility for lawyers affect our ability to keep the doors open during business hours?

Generally, there is little—if any—impact on clients when lawyers are given control over their work schedules, because of a lawyer's commitment to ethics and client service. Any problems that do arise can easily be addressed on an ad hoc basis. Reasons to offer flexibility include (1) the amount of revenue generated per lawyer (keeping lawyers onboard increases revenue significantly), (2) the high cost of attrition when accommodations are not made (estimates range from $80,000 to $250,000 for a first-year associate and significantly more for higher level lawyers), (3) competitors for top legal talent who already offer such flexibility, and (4) the fact that happy workers are productive workers.

Unlike the accounting and consulting firms, which have more decentralized management and innovative, "stay ahead of the curve" approaches to business, law practices are resistant to flexibility partly because it's easier to have blanket policies and procedures that apply to everyone than it is to accommodate individuals. Law firms also fear that professionalism, dedication, and client service will suffer if the office is left unattended for any period of time. For example, offices that still resist telecommuting view it as time out of the office and away from work. There exists a great deal of information and research available to demonstrate that telecommuters generally work more because the work environment is more easily accessible. More money is actually made for the firm. Does client service suffer? No, because clients generally deal with their lawyers on the phone, by fax, and increasingly by e-mail. Lawyers can just as easily talk from home on the phone as they can from the office. In our personal experience, we can definitively say that it's sometimes easier and more effective to work from home.

Froggatt Consulting reported in a 1998 article entitled "Telework Participation: Whose Choice Is It Anyway?," alt.office journal, that in a voluntary telecommuting program at Nortel, a communications company, 90 percent of telecommuters reported increased satisfaction, 88 percent reported increased productivity, individual productivity improved by 10 to 22 percent, on average, and ability to work as a team was better in 40 percent of the cases. There is no reason to believe that similar results are unachievable in law practices. (For other evidence and examples, consider *Telecommuting for Lawyers,* Nicole Belson Goluboff's book published by the ABA Law Practice Management Section in 1998.)

What about scheduled appearances such as court hearings, depositions, and so on? Those simply have to be covered, but usually they can be scheduled at times convenient to all. Deadlines are known well enough in advance to allow them to be met. These days, some depositions are even taken by telephone or video conferencing, which can be done from home or on vacation. Hearings are done by telephone appearance. These measures are viewed as appropriate to cut costs; why not for convenience alone?

Recall that every lawyer on the team was hired because the practice believed the lawyer would be a contributor, represent clients well, and generate revenue and profits. Why assume that allowing flexibility will change that? The not-so-subtle bias here is that because a lawyer wants flexibility, that means he isn't dedicated or serious enough, won't work enough, is just a dilettante, and is "not the kind of lawyer we want." Flexibility is much less disruptive to the practice than having a lawyer in lengthy negotiations, long trials, or other out-of-office work. If the practice will deal with real problems as they arise instead of premature fears that may never materialize, there is only an upside to flexibility. It doesn't cost anything except willingness to try it.

A law-school-to-grave association with one law practice is extremely unlikely in today's work environment. Every lawyer understands the need to become "Me, Esq., Inc." This means that lawyers are always analyzing whether their current associations are best for this time in their lives. If the organization's practice doesn't allow the individual lawyers who create it to maximize their personal productivity while giving them an acceptable life balance, the lawyers will find another roof under which to practice. Indeed, when organizations refuse to be flexible, we counsel individual lawyers to move on.

BEST PRACTICE STRATEGIES

- Recognize the need for flexibility and embrace change. Change is the only constant. Being ahead of the game is where the challenge, the fun, and the profitability are. Remember that the tall oak that stands rigid in the storm is often damaged by the wind, lightning, and hail. Be flexible; bend a little to avoid breaking.

- Be proactive. Consider climate surveys, read management magazines such as *Fast Company* to learn what business is doing to retain employees, and talk with your colleagues who manage other firms to learn about the innovative, proactive, and flexible techniques they are using to keep lawyers onboard. Use your time to discover what your lawyers want and offer it before they have to ask. You can be sure that some headhunter somewhere will offer it first if you don't. Join an organization such as People Wealth's Leading Lawyers, designed to share best practice strategies and solutions.

- Institute flextime policies, if you don't yet have them in place. If you have them, encourage lawyers to use them before they burn out or give up.

BEST LAWYER STRATEGIES

- Understand your organization's revenue and cost concerns and work within them. Ask questions. Take the initiative to find a partner within the organization who knows the firm's revenue practices and will explain them to you so that you understand what is done and why.

- Fairly examine your contribution and your needs, as well as the organization's needs, without underestimating or overestimating either side of the equation. Don't ask for more than the organization can afford to give you, but determine your walking points before you negotiate a win-win solution. For example, many firms are willing to let you work fewer hours if you are willing to accept less money. If that appeals to you, negotiate the best deal you can and then be happy with the outcome. You can always change it later if you find it doesn't suit your needs.

- Recognize that your organization has done business in a certain way for a long time, because the senior lawyers were trained that way and believe it is the best way to practice law. Often, they are genuinely concerned for your career and well- being, and are not simply interested in thwarting your requests. Jumping from the well-known frying pan into the less-certain fire is not always the best solution to your dilemma. Negotiate something you can live with. Hire someone to help you negotiate if you need assistance.

- Do an informal market survey and learn what others in your position are being paid for the contribution you are willing to make. This information is available from a variety of sources, such as law school recruiters, legal placement services, surveys in magazines such as *American Lawyer,* and similarly situated colleagues.

- Be realistic and consider the long-term benefits of your present job, not just the short-term issues. A legal career should be a lifetime development project. Try to avoid sacrificing your long-term objectives to short-term concerns.

CHAPTER 14

INNOVATION

Lawyers and practices must engage their right-brain thinking, be flexible, and learn to manage their practices in creative ways. Consider that it might be possible to think differently than you do now.

Lawyers who are creative in their approaches to client problems often abandon that creativity when they approach firm management issues. For example, a marketing consultant told us that she sends proposals only to firms who request them. Even so, it sometimes takes *years* before a firm responds. This conservative, slow-to-change behavior is at odds with the business world and the personal world lawyers inhabit. Junior lawyers in particular have no patience for it, nor do clients.

Many in-house counsel express frustration with the general lack of understanding by law firms about what in-house counsel needs. Outside firms refuse cooperative efforts between in-house and outside counsel, and the individual lawyers within the firm fail to cooperate to provide a seamless level of service. One innovative approach to this problem we like is a national firm's "corporate counsel commitment," a program designed to address previously identified needs of corporate counsel clients by "partnering" with them. The program is designed to reduce legal costs but is also intended to provide the level of legal services the clients need and want, rather than the services the practice decides to provide. The plan has innovative features such as assigning a client service lawyer (not involved in the project) who will assure high-quality work and deal with fee questions, timeliness issues, and so on. A written plan is promised, as are budgeting and status reports, flexible staffing, and technology integration arrangements. The commitment is formulated after asking focus groups of corporate counsel how the firm could better serve their needs. Following information learned there, the commitment was designed to shift the firm's mind-set to the relationship between the firm and the corporate counsel client, rather than service to an anonymous corporation.

Similar innovative techniques that work for lawyer retention can be discovered by mining the practice's talent. Learn what lawyers want and try to design practices around the lawyers' individual needs. The greatest recipe for success is to match the worker to the work. What you want is work that is self-reinforcing. Self-reinforcement is stronger than external reward, in part because you are attempting to create a lawyer who will, by definition, be self-motivated.

For example, a lawyer who cannot comfortably sell himself should never be a solely responsible rainmaker. Asking him to generate new clients to justify his total salary will not work and ignores the contributions he can make to the firm in other ways. Perhaps he's an excellent technician or a workhorse, and the firm has other talented rainmakers. Pairing them together and making each one's income dependent on the other makes more sense. Remember, your most important asset is the worker, not the work, and you need to nurture each worker's talents.

Celebrate winners without creating losers. Give each lawyer an objective measuring stick that isn't dependent on competing with her colleagues. Create situations in which lawyers can be successful at their work and feel good about it, and there will be self-reinforcement. Ask the lawyers to help create these projects. Responsibility for training and experience can be squarely put on the shoulders of the lawyer, or it can be a shared responsibility between the lawyer and the practice. Despite the proliferation of large law firms, a law practice succeeds by the quality of its lawyers, not the quantity. Given the stakes for both lawyers and practices, it makes little sense to suggest that the responsibility and reward should go to one or the other alone.

Motivation is the one aspect of the equation that is elusive. It has been suggested that the answer to the question of how to motivate people is simple: you don't. What you do instead is to find what already motivates them and use those motivators as appropriate rewards. If this is not the only answer, it is at least the easiest answer, and again, the easy way is always best.

Marshall J. Cook's *10-Minute Guide to Motivating People* contains a number of good ideas about motivation. Contrary to the way most lawyers are taught to think, Cook suggests that instead of identifying the problems in any situation, good leaders should play "angel's advocate," not "devil's advocate." Ask: "What's right with this lawyer? How can he be better?"

And don't forget Pavlov. Reward what you want. To be effective, a reward should be linked to specific performance, timely, and frequent. Innovation can serve you well here, too. Year-end bonuses or profit sharing are not frequent rewards. They are not immediately tied to performance. Innovative, effective, and immediate rewards must be appreciated as well. A lawyer who is embarrassed by public acclaim will not feel rewarded by being singled out at the partnership meeting and asked to take a bow. Work against a fixed scale of rewards, not against your teammates. Earn the points and get the reward without taking anyone down in the process.

Best Practices design and redesign innovative "cafeteria style" benefit and compensation packages that give lawyers control over their quality of life and allow design of an individual approach to meet needs. Ideas currently in use in law practices include these:

- A compensation structure that allows the lawyer to decide how much she makes
- Ten paid hours per month for volunteer work
- A "splash" program that allows a lawyer five weeks paid time off after seven years of service
- Periodic sabbaticals
- Subsidized after-hours and overnight child care
- Dry cleaning or personal concierge service
- Reciprocal free legal services
- Employee assistance programs
- Casual dress whenever a lawyer need not appear in court

All these benefits, and more, have been offered in the business world to retain good employees. Indeed, one small employer made national news when he offered all fifty of his employees—from entry-level draftsmen to administrative assistants—a new 1999 BMW 323s. These benefits (even the car, through innovative leasing arrangements, believe it or not) and countless others can be offered at all law practices for very little cost and with a great deal of gain in lawyer satisfaction.

Lawyers often come to us with a list of complaints, but very rarely see potential for satisfying solutions to their concerns. Instead of this "no-win" perspective, make it a point to be aware of innovations in the business world, because business benefits are the lawyer's option and the firm's competition. Business is where a lawyer's clients and friends work. Best Practices know they can no longer lag behind in their overall approach to lawyers' concerns.

One junior lawyer expressed his dissatisfaction with practicing law by pointing to the archaic way his firm treated associates:

> *In business, employees get a flexible schedule. If my friend needs to be at a soccer game at 4:00 p.m., he can start work earlier and leave when he has worked a full day. At our law firm, you have to be the first one in and the last person to leave or they think you're not dedicated. I can't have a life.*

Another lawyer we interviewed, who was highly regarded by her firm, announced she was leaving the practice of law to return to school and get her MBA. She had been a top law school graduate, was well-liked among her clients and peers, and spoke several languages, which the firm desperately needed to develop its international practice. She started at the firm working for the international law partner, who was notoriously abusive to associates in general, and women in particular. As might be expected, she hated practicing with the partner. She also was very interested in computer technology and was constantly thwarted in her attempts to automate her law practice and help her clients automate some of their legal work. After almost two years, one of the other partners in the office gave her work and provided her an alternative to working with the international partner, which could have been done after two months or less. By the time the change was made, the lawyer had already determined that she could not meet her goals in the practice of law. She surmised that business school would provide her with the opportunities she was seeking for innovation and control over her work. She wanted to "create," and believed this couldn't happen in a law practice.

Practices must be innovative and meet the growing requirements of all lawyers for fulfilling careers so that lawyers need not look elsewhere for fulfillment. Lawyers recognize they will spend two of every three waking years at work and want to love what they're doing. Innovation by lawyers and practices provides lawyers with a way to meet their individual needs and concerns.

BEST PRACTICE STRATEGIES

- Rethink your approach to managing your firm. Rotate creative lawyers on your management team. Never say no. Ask, "How can we make this work?"
- Be aware of what the business world is doing to retain and develop employees. This is often a good indicator of what works to engage lawyers at your firm. Just because it's done in business doesn't make it better, but it doesn't make it automatically wrong, either. The business press is very open with its current practices and policies. Many Web sites explain current trends. Magazines such as *Fast Company* are good for letting you know what growing businesses are doing right. The ABA's *Law Practice Management* magazine and other publications contain many, many suggestions based on good business practices.
- Don't dismiss creative suggestions as too expensive. Often, there is a fairly inexpensive way to achieve creative results. Think "out of the box." Every firm has innovative thinkers within it. Learn who they are and give them the autonomy to find creative solutions to issues that beset the firm. Try innovative approaches. There is no failure, only feedback.
- Be aware that real change begins in the trenches when a small group tries something new and succeeds. Success breeds success. Seek opportunities to start pilot programs for innovative work. This is particularly effective with marketing skills. For example, get the best firm marketers to train other small groups of lawyers and then publicize their efforts. Once others see success with a pilot, they will want to try it, too.

BEST LAWYER STRATEGIES

- Be aware of your own creativity. Often, lawyers decide that their concerns and goals are silly and would not be respected by their peers. Take a chance and gather some data. You might be surprised by how easy it is to approach your colleagues. They may have similar concerns.

- Engage in creative, right-brain thinking. Forget logic, at least while you're considering possible solutions.

- Start with the dream and work backward, instead of trying to create what you think is possible from what you believe you presently have to work with. That is, think of what you'd like to have first. Then figure out how to get it. This is a more creative approach and assures that you will have something you want when you're finished. Working from what you believe is possible is limiting and will keep you from larger accomplishments. This is particularly true of lawyers who are trained to think negatively, postulating "the worst-case scenario" and then designing ways to avoid it.

CHAPTER 15

GENERATION X

Managing Generation X presents its own challenges, but those challenges are equally present in Baby Boomers. The résumé building and learning characteristics of Generation Xers supply creative management solutions for all lawyers.

Like many other management issues, a great deal has been written about Generation X—those Americans born between 1963 and 1981—and how that generation affects work life today. Generation X lawyers are those who began graduating from law school in or about 1988 and will continue to graduate, in the ordinary course, through 2006. It may be no coincidence that the National Association for Law Placement Survey results reported in early 1998, which studied graduates from 1988 through 1992 and therefore focused primarily on Generation X associates, reflected the kind of challenges presented by Generation X in business generally.

A lawyer himself, Bruce Tulgan wrote the book, *Managing Generation X*, which takes a look at the often bewildering and bewildered "Xer." One conclusion seems particularly poignant to our work: "If managers treat Xers as an expendable resource, don't be surprised if Xers treat work as an expendable relationship."

This seems like such an axiom for work life in general, we wondered why Tulgan felt the need to write a book about it. But then we noticed that he had been employed by a Wall Street law firm before leaving to start a consulting firm called Rainmaker, Inc., a self-described "think tank for hire." Could Tulgan's law firm experience (so much of his book is a mirror of law firm life) have inspired him to seek out Xers in other jobs and encourage management changes based on his interviews?

If we focus on associates, the available talent pool for eighteen years will be Xers. These Xers will move into middle management in law firms (to be replaced by Generation Y). We suppose the hope is that once they become eligible for partnership, Xers will have changed everything about the way they think so that they will be willing to live the life of a law firm partner as partners have developed over the past fifty years. This is an unrealistic view that jeopardizes the future of firms.

Midlevel partners, the so-called "Baby Boom" generation or "Boomers," are not all that happy with the status quo, either. It is a rare week when the announcements in the local papers don't reflect partners who have moved across the street. We know of partners, with their firms for over thirty years, who left those firms to join other local practices, to start their own practices, or to take judicial appointments. Their reasons, our interviews suggest, are similar to the ones Xers give for moving on: impatience with outmoded business practices, frustration with inflexibility, lack of challenge in the work, dissatisfaction with their current jobs, and a belief that "life is too short for this." As one twenty-year-lawyer-turned-consultant said:

I just thought twenty years was long enough to do anything.

Much of what Xers complain about are the same matters Boomers complained about as new lawyers, too. For example, Xers are looking for a team where they can make a meaningful contribution. Boomers did, and still do, want the same. Xers want sufficient access to information. Doesn't everyone? Xers want entrepreneurship, defined as room in the work to define problems, develop solutions at their own pace, and produce their own results. This is the very essence of a lawyer's work for her clients. Xers want personal attention, mentoring, and personal loyalty. All successful lawyers feel the same. And Xers seek "security," meaning the ability to monitor and control the success rate of their performance, work status, and return on their investment. No lawyer would feel otherwise, regardless of her position in the firm. Boomers stayed with firms in large numbers at least through partnership. After partnership, they've moved on. Xers are demonstrating daily that they will not sacrifice themselves for the organization, even for a few years.

Seek to provide an environment that the Xer knows is good for him—where he can thrive and be successful. One Xer told us of a recent conversation with his wife about his current law firm job:

She asked me where I expected to find a better boss than the one I have. I know I won't find someone who is so good to me, who takes such a personal interest in me. It will be a real challenge. I've had real opportunities here that I doubt I would have had anywhere else. I could have made more money being a waiter at the upscale restaurant I was working at, but this job has given me great experience and will help me as I move up.

Many law firm compensation systems reward individual revenue production disproportionately to goals in other aspects of management. Training, recruiting, mentoring, marketing, and career building are all expected to be done in addition to revenue generation, making law firm life encompass all the available time in each week. As lawyers mature from inexperienced associates to more senior lawyers, they also mature in life. As people first, lawyers are confronted with biological clocks, health issues, care of aging parents, and retirement planning. Time becomes a more valuable and limited resource that mature lawyers resent selling for mere personal income. In large law firms, lawyers deal with these issues by becoming senior partners who leverage the time of younger lawyers into profits that can be divided among shareholders. Recently, a fourteen-year lawyer in a highly leveraged firm complained about senior lawyers taking a disproportionate share of the firm's profits:

> *I think we need to increase our leverage. We have twenty-two partners and fifty-three associates. But senior partners are taking out so much money, I could do a lot better if I took my business and opened my own shop. For profitability, we need more associates and fewer partners.*

Even assuming the validity of the analysis (which we dispute), where will those extra associates come from? For the first time in history, a generation is substantially smaller than the generation before it (76 million Boomers versus 44 million Generation Xers). The number of workers aged thirty-five to forty-four will decline 5 percent between 2001 and 2005, according to U.S. Census Bureau data. The Bureau of Labor Statistics predicts that the number of jobs available to top executives and general managers will rise 10 to 35 percent by 2006. Law office recruiters bemoan the shrinking talent pool. More important, why would Generation Xers accept the leveraged lifestyle? Unless firms can answer this question, there will be no increase in leverage, and new methods for increasing profitability must be found. If firms aren't careful, the junior rainmakers—like the lawyer we quoted—will leave, too.

Generation Xers seem to understand the value of a dollar and they want more of them. Many Xers have made substantial sums of money by breaking rules and doing things their own way. Boomers who made millions in their twenties include Steve Jobs and Michael Dell, well-known business successes. Bill Gates, at this writing the country's richest self-made person, has a high-school education. *The Providence Business News* reported that 80 percent of Americans trying to start their own businesses today are Xers between the ages of eighteen and thirty-four. Bob Weinstein said in an article for the *Tampa Tribune's* January 31, 1998, edition:

> *The remainder of the '90s promises a new work ethic in which career transcends power and wealth and is bound to personal satisfaction, responsible products or services an altruism. . . . [T]he '90s professionals are quieter and more philosophical about the wealth-producing process. . . . [T]hey're leery of overspending and concerned about socking money away for tomorrow. They realize job security is a myth. . . . They're weary of the present and intent on preparing for the future. . . . [They] make intelligent choices based not solely upon money, but upon gratification and satisfaction. These are the bedrocks of a fulfilling career.*

Thus, if the idea is that to have a fulfilling legal career, one must rise to the top of a law firm so that one's position is sufficiently leveraged to generate income off the time of junior lawyers, what is likely to happen is that those junior lawyers will leave the firm for a more gratifying and satisfying career. And they will make money along the way, while saving more of it than the Boomers did. In short, the current pyramid structure will crumble when the base of Xers walks away, unless the Xers can be convinced to stay in the environment for reasons unrelated to the money they expect to make. And the same is true of more senior lawyers. The advent of Generation X has done nothing more than to highlight and elucidate the concerns of all lawyers. Understanding and accommodating Xers is one key to building a successful practice for all lawyers.

BEST PRACTICE STRATEGIES

- Treat each Generation X lawyer as first and foremost an individual. Create a work environment where each lawyer will thrive.
- Take a hard look at your compensation structure. Does it reward behaviors the firm wants to encourage? Or does it only reward working long hours and collecting the bills?
- Create the type of encouraging, challenging environment Xers thrive on, because Boomers will thrive on it, too.
- Assign career coaches to Xers. Meaningful and constant feedback is one aspect of work on which Xers thrive. They want to continue their résumé building and will seek opportunities to do so elsewhere if your practice doesn't provide them.
- Create products your firm can sell in lieu of time.
- Recognize the practice has a responsibility to its lawyers. Xers know this and will expect the practice to deliver. Xers will not sacrifice themselves for the firm.
- Do not resist the "entitlement" mentality. Work with it instead. Xers *are* entitled to an exciting, fulfilling practice. All lawyers are. Figure out how to deliver it. Everyone will benefit.

BEST LAWYER STRATEGIES

- Define your fantasy job, and determine whether you have the skills to do it. If not, determine where you can get those skills and how far your fantasy will take you.
- Recognize that just as your firm has a responsibility to you, you have a responsibility to the firm and clients you serve. What are you doing for those clients?
- Remember that others are affected by your behavior and performance. Not everything is about you. You are part of a team. Act like it.

CHAPTER 16

ABUNDANCE OF GRADUATES

Graduating significant numbers of lawyers, many of whom have difficulty finding jobs out of school, does not mean that we will have a large number of productive partners in our law firms ten years hence. Indeed, associate attrition statistics and the declining population suggest just the opposite.

We frequently hear that one of the reasons for low job satisfaction among lawyers is that there are just too many lawyers. We're told that the law schools have a profit motive for admitting and graduating too many students and the large national firms could simply eliminate their recruiting programs, because they get so many unsolicited résumés that they don't need to spend time and money looking for lawyers. Yet, at the same time, clients tell us that lawyers do a poor job of delivering legal services and they still can't find competent, affordable lawyers in any specialty. Lawyers tell us they have a hard time finding competent referral lawyers. And many, many lawyers are so busy they find their lives totally out of balance.

Is this an irreconcilable paradox? Actually, we believe "too many lawyers" is a myth of long-standing duration, repeated so often that many lawyers and the lay public believes it to be true. Let's examine the statistics. The U.S. population is now in excess of 270 million, about 1 million of whom are lawyers (and some of that 1 million do not practice law). This means that there is one lawyer for every 270 people in the country, not all of whom need legal services. However, corporate clients, most of whom consume large quantities of legal services, easily dwarf the lawyer population. Recent National Association for Law Placement statistics show that if all the top firms are willing to hire only the top 20 percent of law students from the top 20 percent of law schools, most firms will fall significantly short of their hiring goals, because there just aren't enough top students to go around.

We do not actually know any good lawyers who have too little business. Do you? Indeed, a busy solo practitioner told us:

> *Lately, I've started working more from home. I have plenty of work and usually too much. When I start to get overloaded, I increase my fees to discourage new clients.*

What exists in reality is more work than most lawyers can handle at any given time. Therefore, the number of lawyers graduating from law school only improves a law firm's *potential* for hiring and retention. Society will always be in need of good lawyers, as it has been for the past 2,000 years. As the world becomes more complex and international, the need for competent counsel increases daily. Sophisticated clients will always need good lawyers to handle increasingly complex matters and individual clients need lawyers for basic services.

The abundance of law school graduates makes it possible for practices to attract, hire, and keep the best of the best of the lawyers available. Clients and business needs demand it. As a law practice becomes larger or more specialized to meet the needs of its clients, the practice must have smart, effective lawyers who "fit" and are happy, productive, and profitable, as well as constantly achieving practice goals and enhancing the reputation of the firm and its individual lawyers. By eight years out of law school over 80 percent of lawyers have left at least one law job. At the eight-year point, most lawyers are highly profitable, well trained, and independent workers, who are often responsible for generating business. Hiring new graduates to replace lawyers leaving does not compensate the practice for the time, training, experience, and knowledge of the departing lawyer. As discussed elsewhere, the lost revenue associated with the loss of an eighth-year lawyer is clearly not made up by hiring a new recruit. Indeed, the senior lawyer's expertise is irreplaceable.

Additionally, all the training a lawyer has received in the first eight years is lost when the lawyer walks out the door. Although firms generally don't attempt to capture and quantify the lost opportunity costs of that training, the costs are still incurred. The midlevel associate is often the lawyer who is providing training for more junior lawyers, and that level of training is lost or left to busy partners when the midlevel associate leaves. Client relationships developed by the departing lawyer are difficult, if not impossible, to reestablish with a new lawyer. Also, the firm's culture is negatively affected by the revolving door of good talent.

Practices must be cognizant of their reputations for retention among the legal community. A firm that develops the reputation that lawyers rarely stay longer than two to five years causes the legal community and the law schools to question whether the firm is a good place to work. Once a practice gets a reputation for being a "revolving door," no abundance of graduates will enable the firm to attract the best legal talent the market has available. A law firm can end up being filled with "about-to-retire" lawyers or those who simply cannot go elsewhere.

One lawyer we interviewed was at the top of her class of lawyers and had just made partner. She left her firm shortly thereafter to become in-house counsel for a large corporation. When asked why, after she worked so hard to become a partner, she still chose to leave, she said:

My challenge was to become a partner. Once that was achieved I looked around to see what road was ahead. Most of the partners ahead of me were miserable. The really great lawyers had left the firm and all that was left was a group of mediocre lawyers. I thought if I stayed, I'd become mediocre, too, since that was what was rewarded. So I left to find challenges and growth that I couldn't get at the firm.

Many a previously well-regarded firm has closed its doors when all the best talent dwindled away. No matter how many law school graduates exist, those firms will not be restored. Successful lawyers are "a long time in the making." Don't lose good lawyers before your firm gets the full benefit of their potential, just because you think there's an abundance of graduates.

BEST PRACTICE STRATEGIES

- Recognize that restricting the practice of law to a "chosen few" is impossible, illegal, and not in the best interests of lawyers or clients. Monopolies and restraint of trade are not favored in this country for very valid reasons that apply to law practice, just as they apply to other businesses.

- Treat all lawyers in your firm as the assets they are. Behave in a manner that makes everyone feel valued. Don't treat your lawyers like interchangeable chairs, giving the impression that if one leaves you'll just hire another to replace him.

- Consider the abundance of law school graduates a positive factor in your practice development. Discover how to maximize it.

- Help lawyers develop successful law practices so they don't feel threatened by the "competition" from "too many lawyers."

BEST LAWYER STRATEGIES

- View competition from an abundance of lawyers as a challenge to make yourself stand out in a crowd. Having fewer lawyers available would not increase your business if potential clients don't know about you.

- Develop your referral network. Often clients have legal needs that can't be met because they can't find the right lawyer. Help your clients find lawyers to meet their needs and ask colleagues to refer clients they can't service to you.

- Spend your time perfecting the craft of lawyering, determining which clients you want to serve, and letting them know you're the best lawyer available to meet their needs. You will have all the business you want, even if there are "too many lawyers."

CHAPTER 17

FINDERS, BINDERS, MINDERS, GRINDERS

Practices should recognize that all four types of lawyers are necessary to make the firm productive and profitable. Focusing on finders will ensure the firm has plenty of work. Ignoring the other categories will ensure dissension, dissatisfied clients, and reduced production capacity. Developing plans to value and retain binders, minders, and grinders will enhance the practice. Recognize that the top-of-the-pyramid partners may no longer have the client control the firm assigns to them. A minder, who is often viewed as dispensable, is the true client contact and the lawyer the client views as "mine."

It's hard to say what a law practice "should" look like or what the optimum contribution of individual lawyers "should" be. Psychologists tell us that all humans in our culture have one of four communication styles: thinker (analyzes facts), intuitor (develops good ideas), sensor (takes action), or feeler (senses and uses emotions). Studies show that most groups contain all four styles and, indeed, that group dynamics require all four to be effective. Sensors and feelers probably make the best finders. Thinkers are good minders and grinders. Intuitors may be any or none of the four types of lawyers, depending on whether they just have good ideas or actually do something with their ideas. Maximize each group's strengths and minimize weaknesses.

In many law firms today, a significant emphasis has been placed on marketing. Rainmaking skills are both prized and rewarded. As a lawyer progresses in her career, she is expected not only to be a good lawyer but also to generate work both for herself and for others. Frankly, the "finder model" of compensation systems rewards business generation as if generating the business was the only goal.

There are two sides to the practice of law. One is having good work to do, certainly. But the other side of the practice is doing good work. A new piece of business is just that. It isn't revenue until the work is done, billed, and collected. Rewarding the finders alone will not generate revenue.

Thus, just as in group dynamics generally, law practices need lawyers who will do the work and do it both timely and well. Finders are always out of the office—networking, speaking, and heading committees. Who is in the office handling the client's concerns? Minders. Who is doing the work? Grinders. Who is keeping everyone together? Binders.

At the same time, requiring skilled and talented finders to bill as many hours as grinders is a misuse of talent. Asking introverted minders to become rainmakers is often abusive. Some people—grinders—just like to work. They close themselves in their offices and churn out the product. Encourage and validate all these groups and elevate none above the rest. Acknowledge your personal style and work to perfect it and improve your weaknesses, or partner with another lawyer whose personal style complements those weaknesses.

A fifth-year associate in a national firm was told she wouldn't be considered either for equity or nonequity partnership: *"We don't see you as a first-chair lawyer. You don't take ownership of your cases."* This lawyer billed 2,400 hours in the year she was given the message. She had developed a niche practice, had a great relationship with clients, and generated significant revenue. Yet the firm didn't value her contribution enough to offer her partnership.

Every lawyer is a mix of these four styles, with one less pronounced than the other three. Yet asking every lawyer to perform every function is asking for a room full of portable practices that are independent from the firm. The practice of law may be the only business where the individual lawyer is expected to do it all: sales, production, delivery, management, billing, and collection. Many lawyers are jacks of all these trades but masters of none.

New business origination is heavily weighted in compensation plans, but the methods for keeping track of generating new business from existing clients are less exact. Even less specific is the firm's understanding of the efforts and successes of lawyers who generate new business from existing clients—the minders. Recognize, long before it's too late, that to the client, the minder is really the client's lawyer.

Minding clients might also be termed "mining," because it is from the day-to-day contact with the client that the lawyer learns of additional business opportunities. It is also this daily contact that cements the relationship. Unless the rainmaker is vigilant in maintaining the client relationship (which then takes her away from her highest use—finding more work), the minder is often the only contact between the client and the firm. This relationship develops into a new client relationship with the minder. If the minder leaves the firm, the client is close behind. Clients, like spouses, really can't be "stolen." Rather, they choose to go with the lawyer who does their work.

Yet, in valuing the contribution of individual lawyers, firms often discount the role of the minder. Minders are seen as dispensable. They are the firm's technicians—the less senior, or less gregarious—of the firm's talent. These are the people who get the most work done and contribute significantly to gross revenue. They are the clients' lawyers.

The National Association of Law Placement reports in *Employing Associates in 1998: Patterns and Practices* that there have been substantial increases in both entry-level (15.8 percent) and lateral (26.4 percent) hiring since 1996. The increase in lateral hiring means there is a corresponding rate of attrition from the practices where such lawyers held jobs. Assuming a voluntary resignation in each case, this means that the firms where these associates worked functioned as little more than postgraduate education centers. When the lawyers left, they took their enhanced training with them—and probably a few clients or future client contacts.

Corporate legal departments and governmental agencies recognize the technical expertise of minders and hire them for that expertise. Obtaining clients is not usually a requirement. Work, for the pure perfection of it, can be celebrated. Well-trained and talented minders are highly sought.

This fact alone should be a wake-up call to law firms who celebrate minders as associates—because associates are expected to work hard, are not compensated based on new client generation, and usually need to be "fed" by the partnership—but discount their abilities as partners. Not long ago, a senior partner and his three associates left a large Detroit law firm after over thirty years. His specialty area—employee benefits—was highly technical. It is unlikely that the firm will easily replace him, even though the majority of his work was done for clients of his partners so he was not viewed as a "finder."

Indeed, one chief advantage to practicing law in association with others is the built-in referral network of partners with whom one will share the referred revenue. When sharing the revenue doesn't materialize, the incentive for accepting and referring work from one's partners evaporates. Make sure lawyers of every style contribute to their full ability, and that their contributions are appropriately rewarded.

BEST PRACTICE STRATEGIES

- Recognize the need for minders, binders, and grinders, as well as finders, in your practice. Each has a valuable place within the practice and should be rewarded accordingly. Your lawyers are your best clients. Treat them that way.

- Encourage each type of lawyer to develop strengths and focus less on weaknesses.

- Identify who the client views as its lawyer. This is a good test for value in compensation programs. Minders should be paid as the valuable contributors they are. Even if the firm wishes to reward new-client generation, new-business generation from existing clients should be equally valued.

BEST LAWYER STRATEGIES

- Find something you love to do—something for which you feel passion and happiness. You'll perform better and be more satisfied with your life. Your partners are your best clients. Treat them that way.

- Continue to put the client first. Clients want lawyers who show a real interest in them and their matters. Develop client loyalty and you will always have a successful practice in your current job or in the next one.

- Learn to manage and meet client expectations. Do what you say you'll do, and do it faster and better than you promised, but control your promises. Don't overcommit. Your client should never have to call you and ask for a status report because you will have already delivered it.

CHAPTER 18

VARIABLE COMPENSATION SYSTEMS

Address compensation with flexibility to accommodate all types of individual lawyers and their needs. Elements of fairness, value, and the "going rate" (that is, the rate that keeps the lawyer from going) must be addressed and perceived as appropriate by the lawyers themselves.

One essential issue that all lawyers evaluate to make career choices is compensation. The compensation question has several components, but begins with the inquiry of whether the lawyer is being paid enough to meet her expectations. This inquiry initially is whether she could make more money in other similar firms in her location. The second step is to analyze whether she wants to practice in a different environment. It is the individual lawyer who chooses whether to stay with the firm, and that choice is always made from the individual's perspective. Management's opinion on the adequacy of the compensation system is largely irrelevant to the individual's decision to leave. Assuming her expectations have been satisfied, the compensation question then becomes more complex and concerns issues unrelated to money.

Because most firms have compensation systems in place, the suggestion that offering variable compensation to lawyers will improve retention is viewed with some trepidation. Managers, like most people, abhor change, particularly if it doesn't come with a guarantee. The variable compensation issue also has two sides: What does it take to make the individual lawyer happy? What effect will that have on the other lawyers in the firm? The trick is to achieve both goals. If a practice presently has a retention problem, what you know is that the system in place is not satisfying one or both goals. (If your firm makes fewer than 75 percent of an incoming class partners after the requisite time has passed, you have a retention problem.) If a practice is attempting to prevent future attrition, it needs to find out whether the systems in place are satisfying either goal.

Much has been written about compensation systems in law firms and other organizations, focusing primarily on various compensation methods, criteria, record gathering, and calculation. For example, both *Strengthening Your Firm: Strategies for Success* (Arthur G. Greene, Editor, ABA Law Practice Management Section, 1996) and *Compensation Plans for Law Firms, 2d Edition* (James D. Cotterman, ABA Law Practice Management Section, 1995) address the issues comprehensively. Authors generally concede that no compensation system is perfect. A firm typically has one standard system that is applied evenly, allowing some degree of flexibility within set parameters. The suggested method of dealing with the inherent imperfections in every system is creating one that is flexible enough to survive the firm's changing needs and changing ownership, but continuing to keep one system in place. As *Strengthening Your Firm* explains on page 132:

> *If there is a universal rule with respect to compensation, it is this: Every compensation system works—every compensation system fails. Systems can run the spectrum from objective to subjective, participative to dictatorial. What works in any particular law firm is a system that fits the culture and personalities of the partners. This means that a good compensation system should be flexible to survive the evolving needs of the firm as well as changing ownership. A system must be embraced by the partners, consistent with their collective philosophy, background, and perspective.*

We would add that the firm must have sufficient business and profitability to assure that lawyers can be paid what they believe they're worth in their marketplace, and that every compensation system must allow the individual lawyer some degree of control over his income. The system cannot be one that provides an absolute upper limit for any particular lawyer, but must reward lawyers for superior performance as defined by the lawyer herself. Lawyers, like other Americans, have a disturbing tendency to live beyond their means. If they believe they "need more money," they will look to their current position first, but then test the market. Educate lawyers about financial planning matters to assure that they aren't leaving the firm for financial reasons unrelated to the firm's ability to compensate them.

Lawyers don't work primarily for money. The motives that drive one to become a lawyer and to persevere in the practice are not financial. Indeed, this is true for most Americans. A 1996 *Fortune* magazine survey reported that eight out of ten Americans would continue to work if they were financially independent. This phenomenon is more apparent in lawyers who work for government and nonprofit organizations, perform pro bono work, and accept lower salaried corporate counsel positions. Thus, compensation systems must take into account needs other than money, such as time, benefits, prestige, culture, and so on.

Explaining why she left government service, a sixteen-year lawyer told us:

> *I was very unhappy that my contribution wasn't recognized as valuable. I like to work on a project straight through. I'd work sometimes until three o'clock in the morning. One day my significant other said to me, "Look around. If this was such a great place to be, don't you think it'd be packed right now?"*

*And of course, it wasn't. If I'm going to work that hard, I felt I should get
paid more. Now, my practice is very holistic. I get to see the whole client.*

You need only recall the last five lawyers you personally know who left
their practices for jobs paying less money, or competing judicial candidates in
any election, to recognize this truth. This is not to say that compensation is
irrelevant to lawyers; only that compensation is not the sole motivator driving
a lawyer's decision to devote her considerable talents to any particular organization. A fifteen-year, large-firm partner said:

*People have basic human needs, including to be appreciated and needed.
That's a large part of it.*

Recognize the basic human needs of lawyers and tell them regularly that they
are appreciated and needed.

So, what role does or can compensation play in the lawyer's decision to
stay within a practice? Lawyer interviews reveal four essential criteria:

(1) Fairness (*Is the system fair to me and everyone else, in my opinion?*)

(2) Value (*Does the system value my contribution as I feel it should?*)

(3) The going rate (*Because I can definitely get more money somewhere
    else, what do I need to keep me from going?*)

(4) Control (*Can I control how much money I make, or is that decision
    out of my hands? Can I get what I "need" here?*)

Fundamental fairness is an internal evaluation. Lawyers must feel that the
compensation system makes sense, is applied evenly to them and others, and
takes into account various strengths, weaknesses, and contributions. Fairness
is viewed subjectively as "reasonable," "evenly applied," and "appropriate."
For example, "client control" will not be viewed as a fair measure of compensation if the "billing partner" is not the partner managing the client's
work. Nor will uneven application of any set of criteria be perceived as fair.
Exceptions can be made only if the exceptions themselves are viewed as fair.
Low billable hours by the bankruptcy department lawyers in a year when
there is little bankruptcy work to be had will not be viewed as a "fair" excuse
for reducing compensation, unless low billables result in reduced compensation for others, including the managing partner. On the other hand, such a
decision will be viewed as fair when all partners are subjected to the same
rules.

A system that more heavily rewards new-client origination will not be
viewed as fair by those who primarily originate new matters from existing
clients. Those lawyers must have the opportunity to increase their compensation by doing what they do best. A system will be viewed as "fair" if it was
approved and accepted—in advance of the first application of the rule—by
the lawyers to whom it applies, and if it results in adequate compensation
to each lawyer. In short, the firm must fairly and adequately explain its
compensation system before the lawyer is hired, so that the lawyer later
feels he "got what he signed up for." Changes in the system must also be
approved by the lawyers to whom they apply, not only by the management
committee.

When the firm's method of compensating lawyers is not clearly accepted by the lawyers, attrition problems are sure and certain. A seven-year associate on the eve of partnership said:

> I didn't get a bonus last year, and I had no idea why. I was here every day, did whatever I was asked to do. My clients are happy. Why should I stay with a firm that would do this?

Value, our interviews reflect, can be distilled to one point: Lawyers believe the organization's perception of their individual value to the firm is reflected in compensation decisions. When the organization's perception of the lawyer's value does not match the lawyer's perception of her own value, as reflected in her compensation or in the verbal message delivered with the compensation package, trouble is evident and departure imminent:

> In my second year of practice, one of my colleagues was given a bonus of $500 more than I received. I was crushed. When I questioned my supervising partner about it, he couldn't give me any explanation for the firm's decision. It was obvious to me that the firm felt my colleague was a better lawyer than I was. Right then, my attitude toward the firm began to change. I had billed as much or more than he had, I had brought in business, I was active in firm management. All the things I had been told the firm valued, I did. I couldn't see why my colleague was worth more than I was to the firm.

Two partners left their firms after more than twelve and twenty years, respectively, for the same reasons:

> I just did not believe that there was any basis for distinguishing between me and certain of my partners financially, even with the relatively small dollars involved. I was no longer willing to be treated as less valuable than other partners whom I viewed as less or equally competent.

> All the partners knew that the executive committee viewed me as less valuable than my peers, and I felt that affected the amount of professional respect I received, the extent to which associates and other partners were willing to work with me, and the way I suspected I was being represented to clients. Was all this true? All I can say is, I know how negatively other partners who were in the same position were being viewed and treated. That wasn't how I viewed myself or how I wanted my career to be.

Tell lawyers in advance what their compensation package is going to be and why, and give them a real opportunity to disagree with the compensation committee's decision before it is finalized. Make changes if they seem appropriate, or reach a true win-win solution. Indeed, the administrator from a Washington, D.C., firm told us her firm has one simple rule:

> No one leaves the table unhappy. And we really mean it. We work everything out and we don't have an attrition problem.

Most important to the decision a lawyer makes to stay with the firm or to leave, is what the individual lawyer wants or feels he needs:

I just don't make enough money. The lockstep system we have here means I won't be making enough any time soon. I have a lot of other options.

I make plenty of money. I'd be willing to make less. What I need is more time. But I don't think you can do a litigation practice part-time, and the part-time lawyers I know just end up working all the time for less money.

Your firm must be competitive in its marketplace. There is no other answer to this issue. However, "competitive" in this context is where rewards other than money can be best used. If they trust you, lawyers will tell you what they really want. Is it more time away from the office? Is it a paid sabbatical? There are ways to make your firm stand out in the crowd of "plain vanilla" firms in your market; learn what they are and implement them.

Finally, in Best Practices, each lawyer is able to control her own level of compensation. If new-client origination is a significant factor in the compensation system, the lawyer must feel she can originate clients. Otherwise, she will look for a different system, in a different firm:

I was told that the firm would take care of me. I'd just have to trust them. There's no way I can plan to take care of my family under that scenario. I need to have more control than that.

Best Practices give each lawyer the same level of control over compensation that she would have if she left the firm. This does not mean reverting to a totally objective or formula-based compensation system. Formulas often cause significant burnout and dissatisfaction. They can result in a failure to share profits amicably and do not reward the long-term benefits of continued efforts in marketing, recruiting, and other organizational goals. They do have the advantage of giving each lawyer control over her compensation, but only if each lawyer is charged with "expenses" that are acceptable as well:

I was the head of my department, in a very large firm, and I was responsible for the profit center. But the amount of expenses charged to my department was unfair. I was expected to carry costs that didn't affect my group. It was more profitable to leave the firm and start my own practice. Now, I represent the same clients, work less, and take home more money.

Rather, individual control means a compensation system that allows the lawyer to determine by her own performance how she will be paid. The lawyer must understand and agree with the way her compensation is determined, and she must feel this is the best possible deal she could get anywhere, taking into account all the circumstances. For example, the firm might have several levels of base salary tied to billable hours instead of required billable hours and a set base plus bonus.

Practices that provide and support flexible compensation systems that meet the needs of their lawyers as they mature retain more lawyers. One managing partner told a departing lawyer, *"None of the women lawyers here support themselves."* Of course, she left the firm and has repeated this comment many times. As a woman, would you accept a job with that firm?

The lawyers quoted above either left their firms and went on to other successful work or are considering that option now. The firms have or will lose clients, gross revenue, goodwill, and reputation. In each case, the firms made the same mistake. They failed to provide an individual solution to highly individualistic lawyers.

The question for the firm always is whether some revenue is better than no revenue. Can compensation be adjusted to reflect contribution properly? The answer is: Of course. Any solution that saves the lawyer is worth considering. It's probably worth doing, too. Indeed, in the business world, there is research to suggest that making all employees owners of the business increases employee engagement with the enterprise. Nonequity partnerships, permanent associate status, and of-counsel positions may actually be counterproductive to improving retention.

Each lawyer must view her compensation as fair, appropriate to her value, and sufficient to meet her needs. The only way to achieve this is to discover each lawyer's compensation expectations and meet them, or give an acceptable explanation about why such expectations cannot be met (and prepare to separate gracefully).

Best Practices have systems that (1) are fair and are perceived by the lawyers governed by them as fair, (2) properly value each lawyer's contributions, (3) meet the needs of the individual, and (4) allow the lawyer to control her compensation. The goal is always to ensure the lawyer believes that your organization is the best place for her to practice law at this time in her life.

BEST PRACTICE STRATEGIES

- Before setting compensation, ask each lawyer: What are your compensation expectations this year? Why do you feel you should be compensated in this way? Is there any particular concern you have about your compensation? How can we structure your compensation in a way that is acceptable to you?
- Do not explain that, "One can divide the pie only so many ways," or, "There's not enough money to do that." Instead, ask, "How can we accomplish what you want?" Then do it.
- Consider compensation systems based on performance, not time. There are only twenty-four hours in any day. That cannot be changed. The issue is usually whether you will have some profit or no profit. If the lawyer leaves, you have no profit. Any solution is better than that.
- Consider a cafeteria plan compensation system that allows the individual lawyer total control over what he chooses to earn within certain parameters. If individual hours are falling below expectations, be sure

the reason for low hours is not lack of work. Monitor low hours regularly and learn why they're low before annual reviews cause an impact on compensation.

- Be flexible, creative, and grateful. Remember when you really wanted to hire this lawyer? What are the things about her that do or should cause the firm to feel grateful? There is no valid reason why all your lawyers can't be partners, why all partners can't be equity partners, and so on. The only reason for these decisions is a perception that there isn't enough to go around—not enough money, time, or clients. You wouldn't accept such a proposition from a client; why propose it to your revenue generators?

BEST LAWYER STRATEGIES

- Make peace with your finances and learn to live within your means. Wealth is a state of mind. Develop it and take into consideration other things that are important to you, like rest and relaxation, time with friends and family, and the opportunity to travel.
- Learn your market and your value. Be objective, neither overstating nor understating your value. Why are you worth it? If you can't articulate this to management, chances are they can't appreciate it, either.
- Remember that a private law practice is a moneymaking enterprise and it is your responsibility to make money for the enterprise. If your workload is too heavy, then by all means, take appropriate steps to reduce it. However, if your workload is too light, it is your responsibility to increase it as well.
- Be flexible, creative, and grateful. Remember when you really wanted this job? What things do or should cause you to feel grateful in your current position? There is really no reason why you can't thrive in your current environment. The practice of law is the most flexible profession that exists. You are limited only by your imagination.

CHAPTER 19

RECRUITING AND DELIVERY OF PROMISES

Many lawyers report feeling that they were misled during the recruiting process. Lawyers make an effort to identify their concerns and address them when they take new positions. If the recruiting process is not scrupulously honest, buyer's remorse decreases loyalty and increases attrition, with the commensurate loss of expertise and revenue.

The recruiting process includes not just the formal law school recruiting that results in new-graduate hiring, but also any recruiting that is done for lateral partners and associates through search firms or through individual lawyers encouraging friends and colleagues to join the organization. In every case, representations made to the recruited lawyer must be carefully designed, monitored, remembered, and fulfilled. To do otherwise is to initiate the distrust and dissatisfaction that later corrode the trust in leadership essential to lawyer engagement.

During the recruiting process, the lawyer's competitive spirit is engaged. One lawyer we know would routinely offer recruits whatever was necessary to "close the deal," believing that the practice truly was the best choice for every lawyer and once the lawyer was onboard, all problems could be resolved between people of goodwill. Of course, from the incoming lawyer's point of view, this is deceitful behavior. A lawyer recruited from government service to private practice left the firm after two years. He said:

The hiring partner told me bonuses at the firm exceeded $10,000 and lawyers in the firm made six figures. I took that to mean I would get at least a $10,000 bonus, enough to push my compensation well into six figures. That never happened. As far as I'm concerned, he promised me that bonus. I had other offers that I rejected on that basis. After two years, I wasn't willing to give him another chance.

The more thorough the interviewing lawyer has been in his search for a new association and the more he is giving up in his old practice, the more he will resent the failure to deliver perceived promises made during recruiting. Perversely, even if the lawyer was unemployed when he was interviewing with your practice and had no other offers, he will view representations made to encourage him to join your firm as deceit if they are not delivered.

A firm would not even think about extending an offer to a lawyer who misrepresented himself, however slightly, during the interview process. Firms have withdrawn offers when a law student's résumé lists a grade point average of 3.4, when in fact it was 3.33. The distinction is factually without a difference, but law firms believe that lawyers must be precise in reporting any information about themselves. Yet, law firms regularly make representations in the interviewing process that are inaccurate, putting their "best foot" forward hoping to hire lawyers and have the lawyers adapt to the "real" firm. Often, the recruiting process relies on many lawyers who talk privately with recruits. These private conversations are not recorded and mistakes are easily made, causing the new lawyer to feel misled. Those errors are difficult to mend.

Summer associate programs that present an unrealistic approach to practicing law at the firm are particular problems. The summer interns can come and go at will, and many parties and functions are given in their honor. There is very rarely a serious review of a summer intern's hours, and at the end of the summer, the intern is extended an offer. Law practices know their summer programs are nationally rated and the practice will have problems in the next recruiting season if these summer associates rate the program poorly. However, the practice must recognize that this approach affects the summer intern's expectations of the firm. If the summer intern accepts the offer, he expects to be practicing law in the environment he experienced during the summer program.

At a large firm in Michigan, the summer associates numbered twenty-one. They had very little supervision and were allowed to attend many activities for the "experience," without having to bill their time. A summer associate from one of the best law schools in the nation was extended an offer and accepted. Upon graduation, she joined the firm as a "regular associate" and despised it. She felt as though the real firm was nothing like the firm whose offer she thought she accepted. Worse yet, the firm was disappointed in her. The firm viewed her as failing to pull her share of the load among the other new lawyers. The parting of the lawyer and the firm was very unpleasant, some five years later. She went on to be a very successful in-house counsel at a large corporation with a significant outside counsel budget. She continued to despise the firm and tried whenever possible to convince the other lawyers on the corporation's large legal staff not to send any work there. This "fun" summer ended up being very damaging to the firm's business and reputation.

From the firm's perspective, lateral lawyers who misrepresent themselves and their client base during negotiations will be viewed with distrust by the firm they join. Lawyers looking to move laterally often misstate their projected revenues to get the best deal coming in the door. When the facts do not support the lawyer's representations, the firm feels duped. This breach of trust is very difficult to repair. Both subjective and objective evidence should be reviewed before an offer is extended to be sure the practice and the new lawyer will benefit. The more information each party has about the other, the better off everyone will be.

Another lawyer approached a firm she wanted to join, stating that she had an established expertise with significant clients. The firm was lacking this expertise and hired the lawyer along with her three associates. The firm gave all its existing clients in the practice area to the newly formed group. The group worked hard to cultivate the existing clients of the firm and did not produce the stated revenues they had promised from their existing client base. Additionally, the new lawyers did not fit well into the existing firm culture and were constantly unhappy with management. A great deal of distrust grew between the firm and the group and eventually the group left, along with several other highly profitable lawyers, taking many of the firm's clients.

The potential for disastrous results exists when the law firm and the lawyers aren't careful with each other in the recruiting and hiring process. Best Practices evaluate candidates carefully and make only those representations they are willing and able to deliver.

BEST PRACTICE STRATEGIES

- Be careful about who is involved in the recruiting process, and conduct training every year. Be very clear that any representations must be consistent with the policies of the firm and must be kept. Interviewers should keep specific interview notes that reflect what was discussed during interviews. These notes belong in the lawyer's personnel file.
- Confirm offers in writing and include the specifics of the offer. If the practice has minimum billable-hour expectations, consider putting that in the offer letter, along with other specific information such as vacation time, benefits, and so on.
- Evaluate lateral lawyers carefully. Spend at least as much time evaluating your need for laterals as you would summer associates. Look closely at their work and their client base. A lateral lawyer will affect, positively or negatively, the culture and bottom line of the firm for some time into the future.

BEST LAWYER STRATEGIES

- Closely evaluate the promises made and the impressions you have of the law firms you are considering. Be honest with the law firms and insist that they be honest with you.
- Get impressions of law firms from many sources, inside and outside the firms. Talk with other lawyers, business members, and judges about the firms' reputations.
- Confirm, in writing, any promises that are important to your decision, to be sure you have not misunderstood the offer or the culture.

CHAPTER 20

MAKE GOOD HIRING DECISIONS

Hire lawyers whose goals and aspirations can be met by the practice and who will enhance the practice by their presence.

Recruiting and hiring decisions are one of three key times when a law practice can most easily affect lawyer retention and job satisfaction. (The other two are performance appraisals and whenever concerns are raised.) Most large legal departments and firms of all sizes who hire law school graduates engage in the full recruiting process. Before beginning on this well-known path, practices generally identify their hiring needs and set target numbers of new hires. For example, a firm might want ten second-year students for its summer program and five additional third years for its next associate class. These hiring targets are then passed along to the recruiting committee and the practice goes into action, interviewing and extending job offers. Although there is some effort to sort through résumés and make initial minimum credentialing decisions, the ensuing interview and evaluation process is not usually focused on finding future lawyers who will fit well with the practice's needs. Numerous studies show that a good fit between the person and the job environment leads to career satisfaction, stability, and success. Both the students and the interviewing lawyers in the practice believe they are looking for a good fit, but once the competitive nature of the process is engaged ("How many offers do you have?" "How many of our offers have been accepted?"), it becomes harder to do a good job of choosing an appropriate candidate.

Often, lack of candor in the process is the culprit. How many students, looking for a job, will honestly say they've worked hard for years and want to have a life as well as a career? How many firms will honestly respond that for the first five years of practice, the learning curve is so steep that law must be one's life? Yet if these conversations do not take place, a bad fit is more likely than not.

Law practices often make decisions based on what management believes to be true, without determining whether the assumptions are facts. Many law practices believe that law students or lawyers are lucky to get a job offer, or that the desirability of a job offer is obvious. These practices view the decision to hire as a unilateral one by the practice, and assume the new lawyer will want— and learn how—to "fit in." However, when the expectations or goals of the lawyer and the practice don't match, one or both of them will become dissatisfied with the relationship.

Both the practice and the lawyer have preconceived notions of each other. For example, the firm might assume that a lawyer from Harvard Law School will be very smart and want to work hard. But the lawyer might be burned out from his time in law school and want a relaxed schedule, or he might feel that he's entitled to something more from the firm for his credentials. Often, the practice and the lawyer spend very little time in the interviewing process being honest with each other about their mutual or inconsistent requirements, expectations, or success benchmarks. A few innovative recruiting administrators told us they have compiled data from their existing files about lawyers previously hired by the firm to profile the common characteristics of a successful lawyer at their firms. The effort illuminated the misconceptions about recruiting candidates.

The issue of hiring the right talent is important here. Just as a baseball team wouldn't hire a pitcher when it needs a first baseman, a law practice shouldn't hire the wrong lawyer for the job. Bradford D. Smart, Ph.D., author of *Topgrading: How Leading Companies Win by Hiring, Coaching and Keeping the Best People*, argues that the cost of "mis-hires" is substantially higher than hiring only "A players." Smart suggests (at page 45) that the cost of mis-hires includes not just base compensation, but costs incurred in hiring, maintaining the person in the job, severance, mistakes, failures, wasted and missed business opportunities, and disruption to the practice. Although most law practices would prefer to believe that these costs are overstated, Smart estimates the cost of mis-hires (at page 50) to be between fourteen and twenty-eight times base salary, or an average return on investment of –298 percent to –565 percent. Even if he's overstated the case by 90 percent, that would still make the return on investment at least –29 percent to –56 percent. That is, every mis-hire costs a significant amount of time and money, and takes a toll on culture.

Take the time in the interviewing process to make good hiring decisions. Practices have always considered grades, school standing, law school activities, and other related objective factors as strong indicators of success, and they are. But success is a term defined differently by every individual and practice. Evaluate how the lawyer will fit into the firm culture, how the lawyer will respond to the billable-hour requirements, and other culture issues.

One law firm recruiting team was told to add a female associate to the real estate section. The team recruited and hired three women over a period of five years, only to have each woman become dissatisfied with the firm and her department. Each woman left the practice and the firm for "a better opportunity" within a year and a half, long before she had reached the firm's minimum profitability threshold. What was the real problem here? Were the women all lacking a work ethic, intelligence, or other success factors and destined to be "bad" lawyers? We know the answer is no, because they have all gone on to be very successful in other practices. In this firm's case, the real estate section was populated exclusively by male lawyers who had large egos and competed regularly for how much they could work and bill, not only during weekdays, but evenings and weekends as well. They fought among themselves for clients and work. Associates working within the section felt the brunt of this dysfunctional environment every day.

The recruiting team took its preconceived notions about what the department needed and didn't honestly evaluate the department's and the firm's needs. Ironically, everyone on the recruiting team was aware of the dysfunction in the department. Indeed, the entire firm was aware of the problem, but no one ever dealt with the issues directly. A few years later, after the department lost several more associates, the feuding partners finally separated, leaving a significantly smaller real estate department in the firm. The result of the firm's reluctance to address the dysfunctional department was that thousands of dollars of recruiting and attrition costs, and ultimately client base, were lost.

In this instance, the firm lost a lot more than three very good female lawyers. All these women continued extremely successful careers, and none of them ever referred any business to their former firm or had a good word to say about it when asked. Morale of the other lawyers was seriously harmed by watching the dissatisfied ones come and go. Other lawyers formed negative opinions about the firm that affected cross-selling opportunities, decisions to accept partnership offers, and other firm goals.

Best Practices make honest appraisals in hiring lawyers. This is true for both new lawyers and lateral hires. Does the firm really need an international lawyer? If so, what resources will the firm allocate to make sure that the lateral international lawyer is successful? For example, does the law firm have associates who are willing to practice in that area? Will the lateral hire and the associates be a good match? Best Practices do honest assessments of what it will take to make a new area of business meet expectations *before* hiring a new lawyer, instead of first assuming it will all work out.

Avoid "no-win" situations. For instance, no matter what the new lawyer's credentials are, he will not be successful in an area of the firm that has no work. A firm we interviewed hired a highly qualified lawyer to work in its healthcare section. The lawyer was constantly frustrated because the healthcare partner did the sophisticated work. The facts were that although the firm once had a thriving healthcare practice, the work had been steadily declining. The firm had not recognized the decline and, therefore, had not committed any resources to reverse the trend. This junior lawyer was destined to remain frustrated and would eventually leave, always believing that the firm either did not like her personally or hadn't been honest with her when it hired her. In fact, the firm had not been honest with itself in appraising its needs.

Best Practices have virtually eliminated unhappy matches between lawyers and their practices by honestly appraising a lawyer's expectations and the practice's needs in the hiring process. Determine the answers to questions such as whether the lawyer wants a flexible work schedule and whether the hiring practice group will allow that; whether the lawyer wants independent authority very early in his career and whether the practice can accommodate him; and whether the lawyer has expectations about the partnership track and whether the track is "guaranteed" not to change before he gets there. Ensure that the various policies of the firm have been fully explained to the lawyer before the offer is extended. Best Practices have also reached consensus concerning their true expectations of lawyers.

Understand that lawyers come to be "unhappy" after a period of time when a practice, often without realizing it, disappoints. To avoid this result, regularly review the lawyer's aspirations or goals when he was hired, and determine whether they have either changed or been met. A lawyer on the interview team should be responsible for determining the new lawyer's expectations and what is important to him. After that, the interview team lawyer should be responsible for following up with the lawyer to be sure his expectations have been met. When practice group hiring is done, a lawyer in the group should be responsible for the new hire's development.

It's been said that lawyers are "bad managers of people." Being a good manager is essential and must start at the beginning of the hiring process because even if the practice does a great job of managing its lawyers, it will fail if the original match of the lawyer to the firm isn't correct. Be forthright and honest about culture, requirements for success, and, most of all, limitations. Ask recruits the hard questions and insist on honest answers. A good match between lawyer and law practice begins with making a good hiring decision.

BEST PRACTICE STRATEGIES

- Recognize the need for "a good fit" between a lawyer and the practice to increase chances for a successful hire. Not all bright lawyers will thrive in every practice.
- Properly evaluate the firm's needs and expectations for new hires, whether law students or laterals. Hire only if you truly have a need or are willing to help the lawyer build a practice. And be sure other lawyers already on the team want to add another lawyer to the group. If existing lawyers feel threatened by the newcomer, chances for success are significantly diminished.
- In addition to evaluating law school grades and similar credentials, look at how the lawyer will fit into existing firm or department culture.
- Answer questions honestly and demand honesty in return. Often, practices are concerned about revealing the more demanding aspects of the firm's culture. If culture issues have caused other lawyer departures or are currently causing lawyer complaints, the way to deal with this issue is to change it, not to try to keep it from recruits and hope for the best.
- Look at senior lawyers in the practice and attempt to identify common characteristics that have made them successful. Consider hiring lawyers with similar characteristics or compatible traits.

BEST LAWYER STRATEGIES

- Be honest with yourself about what you seek in a firm. Explore your short-term and long-term goals. Consider your personal style and try to find a practice that fits you well. A bad fit is worse than no fit. It puts you in a job where you will not thrive and causes you to spend valuable time and energy that are not directed toward your goals.

- Speak honestly with the interviewing lawyers about their expectations and yours. If you can be honest with the lawyers now, then hopefully they will be your future colleagues and partners. The chances for dissatisfaction with the job are significantly decreased if you know the real requirements and expectations before you start working.

- Try to determine what kind of practice you want by exploring all options that interest you. Interview lawyers who have the type of practice you believe you want. Find opportunities to observe them perform. Ask: What do you like about your work and your job? What don't you like about each? What are the three most exciting pieces of work you've ever done? And other similar interview questions.

CHAPTER 21

PROFIT CENTERS

Recognition of existing profit centers and creation of additional ones will make the lawyer more valuable to the firm, increase individual value, and encourage engagement. Training in marketing the individual and the firm will benefit all concerned.

Assuming the firm's or department's management has prepared its strategic plan appropriately, no lawyer is hired unless (1) there is existing business for her to do, (2) she brings business with her, or (3) the firm intends to support her financially while business is developed. She is hired for her expertise, as well as her revenue-generating potential. Thus, every lawyer is a profit center, assuming there are no performance problems. If she isn't a profit center, the firm or department has made the wrong decisions. Unless the lawyer's performance does not meet expectations for capturing time, billing, and collection, the failure of the lawyer as a profit center is always attributable to management, not the lawyer herself.

Assuming gross revenue is there, how much profit the lawyer generates is more a function of the firm's overhead per lawyer than anything else. Because the lawyer's personal income is usually less than the gross revenues she generates if she is properly working, only the improper allocation of overhead to her revenues can negatively affect her profit-producing potential.

Profits are also affected by the organization's failure to staff and equip the lawyer for her job. For example, if she can keep three secretaries and a paralegal busy, the practice should provide them for her, despite the fact that more senior lawyers don't have any assistants. If her time is valued properly, providing her with four assistants will increase revenues and profits.

The key to profit generation by lawyers is appropriate pricing of legal services, appropriate control of expenses in relationship to revenues, appropriate business generation training, and acceptance of business once it's brought to the table. Rejecting business because "we don't do that kind of work here" may be a strategic decision the organization makes. Recognize, though, that unless there is an excellent reason for making that choice (and often there isn't), the lawyer will likely go elsewhere to do the work. This is particularly true if the lawyer's compensation suffers after the firm rejects work that would have generated further profits.

All the arguments we've heard for rejecting work that doesn't fit the firm's business profile generally do not take into account the interests of the lawyer accepting the work or the future trends of the business. For example, a general practice firm we know does primarily defense litigation for healthcare providers, not plaintiff's work. Nevertheless, a good plaintiff's contingent-fee case will be accepted. A junior lawyer wanted to do nursing-home work on the plaintiff's side and concluded the firm would reject her efforts in that direction, so she left the firm. Perhaps the firm would have rejected her clients. But the point is that she didn't explore the possibility because she perceived the answer to her unasked question would be no. She left for a firm that was already doing the work. In this case, the firm's failure to nurture the lawyer definitely cost the firm the associate, and may have cost business the firm would have accepted as well.

An innovative program for retaining women professionals (lawyers, accountants, and consultants) that we've recently come across is the "National Office for Retention" of Ernst & Young, one of the giant "Big 5" international accounting and consulting firms that employs more than three thousand lawyers. The best attributes of this program, and others like it being instituted in the most successful businesses, include (1) a director of retention, who reports directly to the chair, has a staff of eight people, and has the full benefit of firm resources, and (2) events designed to share information about career enhancement, address the life balance needs of women and men, and strengthen engagement or affiliation with the firm. After two years of this program, Ernst & Young has increased its retention of women by 4 percent, more than twice the rate of increase in firm partnership reported by the *National Law Journal*'s top 250 law firms. Perhaps even more impressive is the program's estimate that it has saved the Ernst & Young firm more than $21 million in attrition costs.

The professed reason for the forward-thinking program is that the firm is being hired for longer consulting projects and needed the continuity of its consultants to satisfy clients. Law practices face the same issue. Sally J. Schmidt, president of Schmidt Marketing, Inc., in Burnsville, Minnesota, a company that provides market research, training, and marketing consulting services for law firms, reports:

> *Clients express concern about continuity in representation, or the firm's need to orient its new people to the clients' ways of doing business. Some clients may prefer to have senior associates, familiar with their guidelines yet with a lower billing rate, handle their matters in lieu of a partner.*

One thing Schmidt recommends is to provide associates with marketing training and development opportunities as a method for reducing attrition:

> *Associates understand that client relationships and business development are important factors in their ability to make partner (and money), in most law firms. Yet, they are given few chances to learn how to network, write an effec-*

tive proposal or ask for business. Even inexperienced associates indicate they welcome support and encouragement in these areas—particularly opportunities to learn firsthand from skilled attorneys.

Many lawyers today have no interest in generating new clients and less talent for it. They still have the ability to be a profit center for the firm by doing more work themselves at a profit and by supervising others who also produce a profit. The challenge for the firm, as well as for the individual lawyers, is to recognize that all lawyers *must* be profit centers and *must* maximize whatever talents and abilities they have to do so. Often, no one from management attempts to value the contribution of individual lawyers or sits down with them to discuss the income they are generating and how they might generate more, if they chose to do so.

Many firms have adopted the ABA Guidelines—or other guidelines— related to pro bono work. As a result, firms allocate a percentage of the firm's budget to pro bono activities. Surprisingly, the lawyers who do pro bono work seem to lack the basic understanding that it doesn't directly generate revenue *by definition*, although it certainly improves a firm's reputation in the community and may generate business from other sources. That is, pro bono work is a *cost* that is funded by the work of all lawyers in the firm—a part of overhead. If a lawyer chooses to devote her career to pro bono work, she is not a profit center. She may get great personal satisfaction from the work and, by accepting the firm's pro bono burdens, she may indirectly produce business or allow other lawyers in the firm to produce revenue; nevertheless, she must do some heavy internal marketing to convince her partners that she should get a large share of profits. Pro bono positions are essentially salaried jobs that are a service to society and every lawyer's public duty. They are not profit centers and firms should not be expected to pay for them as if they were.

That said, every lawyer's revenues carry an overhead burden. If the burden is perceived as too great, and particularly if lawyers have little or no control over the amount of overhead allocated to them, they can easily calculate the increased personal income they would make by taking their revenues elsewhere. A former national firm partner who opened his own shop a few years ago told us:

There were years when my compensation was significantly less than I generated by my own hours, let alone the money that was made by others doing work I brought in, because the overhead was so high. Now, I don't have that problem.

An international law partner at one of the nation's best firms said:

We all make a little less money than we could make working in a smaller shop, particularly if we have a good year individually. But it all evens out. Usually, the revenue ebbs and flows and we don't get seriously nicked in the bad years either because our profitability is well managed.

In short, successful lawyers are profit centers, and the most successful practices make sure every lawyer has the opportunity to work profitably.

BEST PRACTICE STRATEGIES

- Recognize each lawyer's ability to make money for the firm. Manage every lawyer's contribution to be a profit center by communicating clearly with each lawyer and devising an individual profitability plan.
- Train lawyers in marketing techniques and help them develop expertise that will bring profitable work to the firm.
- Encourage and train lawyers in networking. Networking is not an inherent skill and needs to be learned. Effective networkers generate more business and develop a higher sense of service to clients and colleagues than ineffective networkers.

BEST LAWYER STRATEGIES

- Accept your responsibility to attend continuing legal education programs and choose those that will teach you first to be a skilled lawyer. Also learn to be a good business manager as a part of your career development. The practice of law is a business, and to be successful at it, you must develop business skills.
- Market your expertise to clients who need your services on a regular basis. Develop a marketing plan and stick to it.
- Learn networking basics. Take classes or model a lawyer whose networking skill and success you admire. Networking is the easiest method for developing business and making sure clients become aware of your lawyering skills.
- Determine your profitability points and enhance them. Eliminate distractions that waste your time and reduce your profitability. Make it a goal to work less and make more money. Once your focus is on improving your productivity, you will waste less of your time.

CHAPTER 22

MENTORING TO INCREASE SATISFACTION

Apprenticeship, training, support, and general enhancement of lawyer value are all essential, but only if the lawyer is committed to becoming a productive partner of the practice. Firm partners should publicize the reasons the firm is an excellent place to work, and should encourage retention.

Although it is frequently repeated that the practice of law "is a business," law practices are slower to change and are rarely innovative in business matters. Nowhere is this more apparent than in the lack of development of men and women in law firms. For example, *Fortune* magazine's 1999 list of "The 100 Best Companies to Work For" reports that the "typical" best company has a workforce that is 44 percent female, and provides benefits such as mentoring programs (provided by sixty companies on the list of one hundred), career counseling (eighty-one companies), unpaid educational sabbaticals (thirty-one companies), and paid educational sabbaticals (seventeen companies). Best Companies have such programs because they have made a commitment to attracting and keeping the best talent, and such programs help achieve that objective. Law firms generally do not have such programs in place and experience substantially higher attrition rates than other businesses.

One big issue in lawyer attrition is "quality of life" or "life balance," addressed elsewhere in this book. Our interviews with lawyers and firms reflect that lawyers leave their jobs due to other factors once the life balance issue is addressed. Such factors make it difficult for lawyers to achieve the level of success they seek from traditional law practice. Chief among these factors is the perceived lack of access to firm leaders or mentors.

Women in particular often have the view that a strong mentor is necessary to help them achieve advancement in their firms. They perceive that men are groomed for leadership positions by more senior, male partners. Women feel they are not given access to clients in the same way as their male counterparts. They also feel that men are groomed to take over rainmaking roles in ways that women are not. Women often perceive that their contributions to the firm are not valued in the same way as men's contributions. Women also believe that the way they want to practice law is not acceptable to their firms. Many women feel these factors make it too difficult to break through the "glass ceiling" and, more important for our purposes, are not worth the effort. That women's career development concerns are disputed or viewed as unimportant by male lawyers is perceived as part of the problem. Indeed, what male management views as "reality" is irrelevant to the point: If women feel they are not excelling in their current jobs, they have many opportunities to work elsewhere.

Our informal results were echoed and expanded by the Catalyst Guide, *Advancing Women in Business,* published by Jossey-Bass in 1998. The Catalyst conclusion, and ours, is that retaining and advancing women in law firms is a challenge that must be met head-on by the firms and the lawyers themselves, in a proactive way. Absent programs to which firms and lawyers are committed, over twenty years of experience have shown that women will continue to flee traditional law practice in favor of forums where they can excel. Formal mentoring programs by bar associations help retain women in the profession and are good places for individual lawyers to find volunteer mentors. Outside consultants who provide individual mentoring at firm expense have proven to be a successful option for individual lawyers. But mentoring programs sponsored and supported by top management are needed to retain women and men in law firms and departments.

Many law firms have mentoring programs that do not achieve the goal of career development for lawyers. A formal program is only as good as the lawyers who adopt it, commit to it, and execute it. Where programs fail is in the level of commitment by the firm to the goals of the program. If there is no budget or reward for the mentors, and if the assignment is viewed as just another task to be done on personal time, only the most devoted mentors will do a proper job. Without a dedicated mentor, the mentee will not make full use of the program. No one wins.

A successful mentoring relationship is one that serves the needs of both the firm and the individual. Often, a lawyer's departure can be delayed or forestalled by consulting with a trusted lawyer who can provide a different point of view. For example, a male partner recently consulted us about leaving his firm for a smaller practice. His rationale was that he could make more money if he continued to generate the same revenue, because his costs would be lower. After discussing candidly the joys and sorrows of small-firm practice, and the benefits to remaining in his current firm (including the mentoring/coaching relationship he has with his senior partners), he decided to stay at least a while longer. The firm gave him more money shortly thereafter, demonstrating that it really did value his contribution in a way that was acceptable to him—he just didn't know it. Lawyers often have viewpoints that can be changed. A senior associate, offered a "counsel" position with her firm but not a "partnership," seriously considered leaving. After talking with us, and examining the benefits to accepting the "counsel" position, she, too, decided to stay with her firm because it was the best place for her career right now. This type of unbiased counseling is available to increase retention every day.

Lawyer retention, at all levels, is critical to the continued viability of law practices, and successful, proactive lawyer retention programs are a wise investment in a law firm's future. Although many firms are not in a position to underwrite the costs of a firmwide retention effort, no firm can afford to ignore retention initiatives. Retention consulting services are available for firms that want to outsource the program or need assistance in instituting an in-house program. Other resources, such as the Catalyst study, are available for firms who wish to create programs. An active mentoring/coaching program can make the difference between success and failure of all lawyers in every setting.

BEST PRACTICE STRATEGIES

- Include heavy emphasis on personal respect and the valuable contribution each lawyer can make to the learning and advancement of others. Everyone has something to add and no one has a monopoly on good ideas.
- Make a commitment to mentoring and advancing the careers of lawyers in your practice. The equivalent of the highest level lawyer in the practice group should be accountable for lawyer retention. The program should have a budget and mentors should be encouraged to spend it.
- Assign committed mentors to the program—people who will take their responsibilities seriously and be active in the career development of their mentees.
- Reward mentors for the work they do in retaining lawyers. Giving monetary rewards if mentees stay at the firm for a set number of years or reach certain milestones would convey the message that the firm values retention and the mentor relationship.
- Award mentors for successful mentoring relationships. Ernst & Young actually gives an award, in a public ceremony, to the manager most dedicated to advancing women in its retention program.

BEST LAWYER STRATEGIES

- Recognize the need for a mentor and take the initiative. As in other areas of your career, you will be most satisfied if you have some control over the process. Be clear about your expectations. Remain alert to mentoring opportunities and be ready to make the first move.

- Try to find a partner or senior lawyer in your organization who will help you advance your career, and find ways to spend more time with her. A request to become your mentor may be rejected because the senior lawyer doesn't have the time, energy, or desire to make a long-term commitment. Instead of requesting a long-term commitment, you could ask (1) to work on a particular matter or committee assignment, (2) for an introduction to a particular contact, or (3) for help with some other specific, short-term goal.

- Pay attention when working with others. Learn from them, regardless of whether they are making a conscious effort to teach you. Ask questions when appropriate and adopt strategies and behaviors that you see producing successful results.

- Be a lawyer others want to mentor. Demonstrate interest and a willingness to work hard, and commitment to the job, the mentor, and the law.

- Develop a network of mentors from whom you can learn a variety of skills to advance your career. Mentors themselves have strengths and weaknesses that you should attempt to identify, emulating only the strengths and avoiding the weaknesses.

- Be willing to let your mentor go. If the relationship is successful, you should surpass her expertise. Although the personal relationship may continue, at some point, you must fly solo.

- Mentor junior lawyers. This helps you by retaining lawyers with whom you like to work. Beyond that, trying to help a lawyer through the "school of hard knocks" boosts your understanding of the current trends among lawyers and how far you've come in your own professional development, and provides insight to your senior lawyers.

CHAPTER 23

UNDERSTAND PRACTICE GOALS

Are partners attempting to build a firm that will be valuable to its clients, the profession, and future generations of lawyers? Or, is the practice a group of lawyers intending to provide jobs for themselves as long as they wish to practice? Identifying the goal of the practice will dictate many of its activities and policies.

It's been said that there are two kinds of entrepreneurs: those who are looking to create jobs for themselves and those who are trying to build businesses to sell them. Law firms can also be divided into two types: those that are jobs for partners, and those that are institutions intended to survive their partners. Each presents different challenges and rewards for Best Practices and Best Lawyers.

A firm started to provide jobs for current partners is substantially different from a firm whose goal is to continue as an institution for future generations of lawyers. In today's market, either type of practice can be successful, but it is necessary to identify the practice's goals to do so. If it stays focused on its goals, a new firm can achieve significant success during the lifetime of its partners and then either join another practice, phase out of business, or attempt to sell the business to other lawyers. By contrast, a firm seeking to become an institution faces other issues. A firm that's been in continuous business for a hundred years can vanish almost overnight, when the current generation of lawyers in midlevel partner positions leave the firm for another practice. A large firm that seeks to become an institution can disintegrate for a variety of reasons; often the biggest issue is that the firm never was an institution but rather a loose collection of lawyers sharing office space.

A firm seeking to provide a satisfying, successful work environment for today's lawyers—without the goal of saving the firm for posterity—will have a sense of immediacy that is lacking in institutional firms. The most successful and common model is the boutique practice, where all the partners do substantially the same type of work, or the lawyers knew each other and worked well together in some prior practice. These practices are usually small; larger practices have a range of seniority among lawyers that reflects the addition of lawyers to the mix over time, and that perpetuates the practice beyond the initial contemplated term.

Changes in small firms are easier to implement because there are fewer lawyers whose consent is required. Economic policies are more easily administered because there is more unanimity of opinion, and often common goals were agreed upon before the practice was started. In today's market, getting business is often easier for the boutique firm and job satisfaction is easier to pursue because of the flexibility and control available to the partners.

Adding lawyers to this type of practice is a challenge because of culture and personal style issues, but often there is little need to do so. Finding part-time, temporary, or contract lawyers to help with occasional increased workloads is relatively simple.

Some of the happiest lawyers we interviewed are solo or small-firm practitioners. Most of them reported common pleasures and perils:

> *I like the control I have over my practice. I still feel the need to get to the office every day by 8:30. Probably my big firm training. I was downsized in the early '90s after I'd made partner in a big firm. Honestly, it's the best thing that ever happened to me. I represent the same clients and do the same work I've always done. I do have more administrative responsibilities now, but I had those as a big-firm partner, too. Now, I do them when I want to, not when the rest of the firm needs me to. I love this practice and I'll probably do it forever.*

> *I worry about finances. I've been a solo for ten years now and I have always done well. I'm particular about the cases I take because I've managed my money well and I have a substantial reserve. I worry though about the unpredictability of my workload. Sometimes, because of the nature of my practice, it's months before a new case comes in the door.*

Best Botique Practices identify and perpetuate the pleasures of small practice while minimizing or protecting against the perils. By doing so, the practice flourishes and satisfies its chief goal: to provide a pleasurable place for lawyers to work, until they no longer want the job.

Institutional Best Practices face different challenges, chiefly related to institutional goals and management. Often, leaders have no business training since initiating managing partner roles, beyond weekend seminars and consultants. As a result of this frame of reference, management committees generally don't have a "team-building" mind-set, or if they do, they don't have any real understanding of how and why to build the team.

Managing partners on management committees are usually practicing lawyers as well. Their popularity with their partners or roles as significant rainmakers are the chief criteria for their positions as leaders in the firm. In contrast, the most successful practices have credible leaders with demonstrated leadership ability, who can lead the practice toward articulated goals.

Like Americans generally, lawyers are fiercely independent. That independence precludes working cooperatively, unless the lawyer can be the leader of the team or at least a major part of the team. This presents a problem for group practice, because team leaders in law firms are usually the senior lawyers who have "client control" over the type of work done by the team. Being part of the team is a role that causes many lawyers discomfort, and they often have little respect for the managing partner's decisions. Two very successful partners in a large, national law firm each told us:

> *I am completely dissatisfied with the management committee and I don't trust them. I don't agree with the decisions they make but I have to live with them. I'm looking around and I plan to leave the firm as soon as possible for that reason.*

Another big-firm partner in a different hundred-year-old-practice said:

> *I will no longer be judged and found lacking by people with less expertise and fewer skills than I have. When is the last time the managing partner did any real lawyering? Why should he be able to judge my work and set my salary? He has no idea what I do for clients. He hasn't even talked to me once this year.*

On the other hand, a highly successful lawyer told us about policies in a firm consistently rated very high in job satisfaction for lawyers:

> *No one knows what anyone else makes except the managers. It keeps the lawyers from getting petty and competitive. You have to have a certain amount of trust in the managers to treat people fairly. The management committee assigns points and 80 percent of pay is based on that. The other 20 percent is discretionary, based on a list of nebulous criteria. We have seven managers from various areas of the firm. I know those guys and I trust them. I think they do a good job.*

Beyond the limitations of management skills possessed by management committees, the financial structure of many firms is not conducive to creating a cohesive business enterprise. Income is related to the revenue generated. The actual revenue collected is divided at the end of each year according to a formula, leaving little to sustain the ongoing business the following year. Indeed, some firms still have partnership agreements that do not obligate departing partners to pay a share of the firm's debt load. This means that if a partner leaves, the remaining partners must shoulder any debt burdens that continue, regardless of the remaining partners' ability to do so.

Lawyer income is closely tied to revenue collection, but some firms have attached a "per lawyer overhead" number to every lawyer, regardless of the partner's ability to sustain it. In many partnerships, there is no such thing as a "salary" and "bonus" structure after partnership or shareholder status is achieved. Compensation is strictly based on dividing the profit pie according to predetermined criteria, or on subjective judgment of the managing partners. At least one large international firm has reposed final decisions for setting every partner's salary with the managing partner, whether he has any real contact with individual partners and knowledge of their work or not. This move has caused more than minor dissatisfaction among partners who feel the system is unfair and too easily affected by internal politics.

For these reasons, and probably many more, law firms have trouble becoming brand name, cohesive institutions with the ability to stand the test of time. As opposed to department stores, law firms closely resemble shopping malls: every store under one roof, all contributing to the overhead of the operation through lease agreements but responsible for individual revenue production and profits. There are common benefits, but no one store is so closely identified with the mall that it can't move to another location and resume business as usual.

This "shopping mall" organizational structure stands in marked contrast to the continuing enterprises exemplified by law divisions of governmental agencies, law departments of corporations, and business generally. In business, there are common goals and team efforts to meet those common goals. Agencies are not required to produce revenue. Indeed, by definition, they spend without revenue generation. Agencies are given a budget within which they must operate, and they have no "upside" potential to increase that budget. The compensation of lawyers within government agencies is less lucrative than private practice, and is totally unrelated to the spirit of capitalism because it is not the agency's purpose to make a profit. Interestingly, the 1997 Florida Bar Opinion Survey reflected that the most satisfied lawyers were judges, federal government lawyers, and local government lawyers. When we talk with these lawyers, they tell us they work hard but have no idea how to measure the value of their work in money. Of course, money is the only measure used by most private-practice law firms.

Businesses in general focus on organizational goals, and law departments are structured to help serve those goals. For example, the purpose of a car manufacturer is to make and sell cars. Everyone works toward that goal and everyone (including each shareholder) is paid based on how much profit finally exists after cars are sold. The legal department of a car manufacturer serves the legal needs of the corporation. The lawyers are not paid for their "billable hours," but for helping the company increase profits by working to negotiate contracts, draft sales documents, supervise the defense of product liability claims, supervise labor counsel, and so on.

Many law firms have no goals beyond providing legal services to certain types of clients. Lawyers share income and expenses in the hope of generating sufficient revenue (1) to support themselves, (2) to provide a congenial atmosphere in which to practice, and (3) to retain a qualified group of lawyers to do legal work that they do not do themselves but from which they can get a share of the fees generated. These are goals shared by every law firm. What makes one different from another?

A six-year lawyer considering changing firms told us she was reluctant to leave her firm because, *"We are the best firm in [our city]."* Now there's a goal that will keep lawyers onboard and distinguish a firm from its competitors. Another lawyer told us he'd accepted his job with an old-line firm because his father had told him, *"They're all gentlemen there."* Our prior firm was known, at the time we joined it, as *"the preeminent management labor firm in Detroit,"* the city where labor law was created.

One identifying characteristic that doesn't mean anything positive to lawyers or clients is the oft-quoted line that a firm is "the largest firm" in a particular city or area, unless the firm is a plaintiffs' personal injury practice or some other type of practice that is typically small in size, and the larger size can be said to be attributable to great success in the field. Nor is it impressive to clients or lawyers that a firm "delivers the highest quality legal services at reasonable cost." Clients and lawyers expect all firms to do that.

Institutional firms can accept the challenge to develop a corporate identity that means something to both clients and lawyers, to create a firm with a common goal toward which all lawyers can work, and to create a team that successful lawyers want to join, stay with, and perpetuate for future generations.

BEST PRACTICE STRATEGIES

- Determine what kind of practice you have and what kind of practice you want. Articulate your goals in writing and gain agreement of all affected lawyers to pursue the goals you select. Publicize firm goals inside and outside the firm to enhance reputation and create enthusiasm.
- Select appropriate leaders for institutional practices—leaders with expertise and the ability to inspire trust in others, and whom others will follow toward firm goals.

BEST LAWYER STRATEGIES

- Understand your firm's goals and get behind them. Be part of the team.
- Evaluate whether you trust firm leaders. If you do, say so. If you don't, try to discover why you don't, and then resolve your concerns. Usually, firm leaders are perceived as untrustworthy due to misunderstandings and lack of information flowing to lawyers. This problem can be solved if you take the initiative to communicate directly with firm leaders and learn why decisions are made.
- Accept only work that fits within your value system and allows you to provide ethical service to clients.
- Read, understand, and adopt the ethical rules of your jurisdiction as a minimum personal code of honor by which you choose to live, regardless of your immediate difficulties. Having a strong moral code gives every immediate problem a clearer answer—even if you'd prefer an answer different from the obvious ethical one.
- Take responsibility for improving the public image of lawyers. Consider the public perception of your conduct as a lawyer. Behave as if you were an ambassador for the profession. Representing clients zealously is not inapposite to a positive public image. "Deny, deny, deny" may be a good legal defense, but it is a poor public relations strategy.

CHAPTER 24

HONEST APPRAISAL AND EVALUATION

This process must be value driven to ensure and inspire trust, without which a practice cannot flourish.

Honest appraisal and evaluation are basic parts of what lawyers provide to clients. Lawyers must analyze and communicate with clients in ways that let clients know that although real problems exist, they can be solved. This process is also key to growing a law practice. Use honest evaluation of the strengths and weaknesses of the practice to move forward toward solving problems and goals.

All aspects of retention analysis and achieving growth require honest communication and "straight talk" in an atmosphere of a common goal. A central part of that communication is trust. Without trust, the practice will not get the honest communication it needs to move forward. Most practices have experienced situations in which various factions within the practice did not trust each other. This lack of trust not only leads to lawyers leaving the firm and important clients choosing to take their work elsewhere, it also causes some lawyers who stay with the firm to thwart its goals. Junior lawyers must truly feel they are valued and their voices will be heard. Midlevel partners must believe that if they refer work to other sections of the firm, referral lawyers won't attempt to disparage them or try to "steal" "their" clients. Honestly analyze strengths and weaknesses in these areas and correct problems by achieving an appropriate balance between lawyer autonomy and accountability. Reward successes promptly and directly; Address problems just as swiftly and directly.

One new lawyer with whom we spoke decided she needed to leave her firm to grow her practice. She had many contacts with minority-owned companies in the construction industry. She believed she had asked her firm to support her

127

in her efforts to attract and increase this business. For the most part, she felt her requests were ignored:

> *When I finally got the firm's attention, the senior construction lawyers set up a meeting with the various construction companies to sell the firm's services. But they didn't invite me to attend the meeting. I decided I would never be able to grow the business without having the senior partners steal the work from me. I left the firm and now have a very lucrative and successful minority construction law practice. My old firm still doesn't have any business in the area, although now they're trying.*

A great deal of information on listening techniques explains why people don't communicate their needs, even when they believe they are doing so. Given the stakes in this situation, we suspect that the lawyer didn't communicate her needs as strongly as she believes she did. It is possible that the senior lawyers just didn't understand her or didn't really listen. In any event, it was not in the firm's best interests to ignore this lawyer's efforts at client development. The firm demonstrated to this associate and others that client development was not really appreciated, and if an associate tried to develop business, the senior partners would "steal" the clients because the firm overly values "finders." The senior lawyers also showed their colleagues their failure to act as "team players" when the goal is getting new business for the firm. All told, the firm preached what was important, but behaved very differently.

In-house lawyers often complain that large law firms are unable to act as team players, but either they don't communicate those needs or their requests are ignored. For example, an in-house lawyer told us:

> *I'm responsible for a large amount of work, but I often need expertise from the outside law firm. They seem to have a difficult time having several partners work with me at one time when no one within the firm has the lead position. Although the firm professes to be a full-service firm, they tend to take a pyramid approach to assigning the work. Additionally, outside counsel often has a difficult time working with other outside firms on my team.*

Best Practices never allow this to happen. Instead, they listen carefully to the client's needs, make an honest assessment of what the firm truly does well and what needs improvement, and then take appropriate action.

Firms generally avoid honest appraisal and straight talk because they find it uncomfortable to hear and deliver. Often, individual lawyers want other lawyers or practice groups to improve without honestly appraising themselves. Lawyers have not been trained in methods for delivering constructive criticism and fear being offensive to others or receiving a defensive response. Lawyers also understand that things are rarely as they seem, and that there are many views on every subject. They are trained to identify and articulate the best argument on either side of any issue. There is also a certain amount of "paralysis by analysis" in most situations managed by a committee of lawyers.

The recruiting partner of a large multinational firm recently told us that the firm doesn't have a retention problem:

Lawyers don't leave until the forth or fifth year and they don't go to other firms when they leave.

This unintentional myopia causes the perpetuation of an erroneous comfort level. Losing lawyers at the fourth- to fifth-year level is a more significant loss than losing more junior lawyers. In this same firm, although the incoming first-year class numbered 135, the class just promoted to partnership contained only 15 lawyers. Such a failure of honest appraisal and insight prevents this firm from improving its retention rates. Best Practices make a more honest attempt to view the realities and address them.

Analyze, understand, and deal with practice issues in a straightforward, nonoffensive, and proactive way. If training is required to improve both the ability to understand and identify problems, as well as to communicate them constructively and obtain agreements for change, practices must seek and provide that training. Ask consultants to help with getting candid feedback from clients on firm conduct as well as work product. Ask lawyers for suggestions and then follow through. Good lawyers recognize their performance can always be improved and they spend time analyzing their own strengths and weaknesses first.

Practices must recognize that in this area, as in most others, trust is essential. Among lawyers of goodwill, all problems can be solved if they are properly identified and then addressed with a willingness to change.

BEST PRACTICE STRATEGIES

- Be honest with your lawyers and yourselves about the firm's strengths and weaknesses. Exploit the strengths. Get a commitment from a task force to deal with the weaknesses.
- Evaluate the firm's current position and where it wants to head before making any decisions. But don't wait too long. Some movement is always better than no movement.
- Be aware that trust is essential. If management isn't trusted by other lawyers in the practice, management must be replaced. The practice is better off with a less-talented manager than an untrustworthy one.

BEST LAWYER STRATEGIES

- Be honest with the firm about your concerns. Nothing will ever change unless the lawyers communicate candidly, openly, and directly with management.
- Control your own expectations. Do some research into what is possible and what isn't. Don't make unreasonable demands, but don't accept unreasonable rejections either.
- Develop an ability to speak plainly without being offensive. Learn about communication styles and the differences between communicators. Be

sure you are communicating clearly and are being heard before you conclude the practice doesn't care or isn't interested in your concerns.

- Trust your instincts, but give the practice a chance to correct problems you bring to its attention. Say, "I am concerned about this issue. I would like to solve the problem this way." If the solution requires permission to proceed, give a deadline and follow up if no response is received. Do not assume lack of an answer is a negative answer.

CHAPTER 25

RECOGNIZE AND ELIMINATE LAWYER DISSATISFACTION

Every lawyer leaves the practice because of some dissatisfaction with the firm. This is true even in circumstances when the lawyer is accepting a "better opportunity," following a spouse to another city, or moving from private practice into government service. If the lawyer was satisfied with the firm, she would not quit.

Every book written about employee advice tells employees not to "burn bridges" when they leave one job for another. Lawyers take this advice to heart. Thus, a firm cannot assume that any departing lawyer will state the real reason for leaving when he goes. There is only one reason lawyers leave their jobs: They believe they will be happier somewhere else. The real issue in each case is whether that belief is true.

Make it easy for lawyers to return after serving a stint elsewhere. One national firm we know has a "club" it calls "The Grass is Browner." It includes lawyers who left the firm, thinking the "grass would be greener" somewhere else, and have now returned after finding they were not satisfied with their new jobs. The "club" is officially sanctioned by the firm and publicized in the firm's formal literature, giving others who are thinking about leaving enough information to evaluate new jobs.

Many law practices deal ineffectively with lawyer concerns. If the dissatisfied lawyer is viewed as a disloyal complainer, it discourages other lawyers from raising honest concerns, but does not eliminate those concerns. Refusing to hear concerns means the practice will have no opportunity to correct them. Loyal lawyers who see problems in the practice raise the issues with the firm's management so they can be addressed.

If a lawyer or a client is unhappy with the firm, he generally doesn't tell the firm, but tells everyone else he knows. Lawyers talk among themselves and with colleagues about their long-time dissatisfaction with the firm; they just don't tell management about it. Tell lawyers and clients, "If you're happy, tell everyone; if you're unhappy, tell us."

Lawyers often perceive a refusal to hear concerns as a lack of caring by management, which in turn causes low morale. Lawyer dissatisfaction can permeate every level of the firm. It will affect productivity, client relations, and firm culture. Clients know when their lawyers are miserable. Dissatisfaction shows in responses to the client and to the client's business partners. Clients who feel that lawyers are always "cranky" will resent them and then stop working with them. Practices with good lawyer retention experience attempt to make their lawyers the most satisfied lawyers around, partly to increase client satisfaction.

Conduct regular focus groups where management members or consultants meet with different combinations of lawyers and ask them about their concerns. Make the questions both structured and unstructured, to get lawyers to speak openly. Asking the structured questions in subsequent focus groups allows the practice to track its progress and to identify new and different concerns. Also, generate and disseminate statistical data to show the practice's progress. Objective progress often helps show the other lawyers in the firm that issues are being addressed and considered by management.

Lawyers who leave their firms to follow a spouse to another city deserve special mention. These situations are often painted as "an offer too good for the spouse to pass up," and despite the lawyer's "complete satisfaction with his practice," the family unit must move on. In every instance where we have investigated this scenario, the lawyer was, in fact, dissatisfied. For example, a fourteen-year lawyer and major breadwinner in the family, unhappy with her firm, said:

> I didn't want to create any unnecessary hard feelings, so I told them my husband was being transferred for a better opportunity. He was being transferred, but it was because we had decided to move and he asked for the change.

Another lawyer recently left his firm to "return" to his hometown. His wife had received an offer "too good to refuse" from her employer. He'd "loved the firm" and "had a bright future" there. The firm was sorry to lose him and helped him make the transition by allowing him to telecommute for several months until he found a new job. Talking with the lawyer, though, we learned the full story:

> One of the partners on my team who was very influential seemed to be blocking my progress. I'm not sure if he was jealous of me or if he felt threatened or just didn't like me. But my mentor would be retiring in the next five years and he would be the head of the department. I just didn't think I should make my future in that environment. When we were weighing my wife's offer against my future at the firm, we decided her opportunity was better than mine.

Invite lawyers to raise their dissatisfactions, and then recognize and address the issues. Lawyer dissatisfaction will negatively affect the firm's culture and its reputation in and out of the legal community. Lawyers who stay, leading lives of quiet desperation, are corrosive to their environment and themselves. With every business becoming more savvy and sophisticated about how it selects legal services, no law firm can afford to ignore the concerns of its lawyers.

BEST PRACTICE STRATEGIES

- Determine exactly how much autonomy lawyers will be afforded and how much accountability they will have. Decide exactly what the rewards and punishments will be for partners, senior lawyers, and junior lawyers for meeting or failing to meet expectations everyone has agreed to meet. For example, don't adopt a blanket policy that fines lawyers for failing to submit time sheets. Instead, deal with those lawyers who routinely fail to submit their time by an appropriate sanction. The message: Failing to turn in time reduces revenue and thus the practice's available cash to pay the draw or distribution of the nonconforming partner. Don't apply sanctions where no problem exists.
- Recognize the costs associated with lawyer dissatisfaction. A happy lawyer is a productive lawyer.
- Discover what dissatisfies your lawyers. Encourage and invite lawyers to raise concerns. Hold regular focus groups and do regular climate surveys to determine your lawyers' job satisfaction levels.
- Address and correct unsatisfactory conditions promptly. When lack of challenge and excitement in the practice are the issues lawyers raise, assist lawyers in conceiving and developing "WOW! Projects" (as Tom Peters discusses in his book, *The Pursuit of WOW!*).

BEST LAWYER STRATEGIES

- Be part of the solution. Be open and honest with yourself and your colleagues about your dissatisfaction, while framing a solution in a positive way. Although mere complaining is nothing more than a self-indulgence, identifying and solving issues that matter to you is essential. Resist the urge to keep your concerns to yourself. Your dissatisfaction will increase if left unresolved.
- Speak out. Take charge of your own career. Communicate your expectations to your management committee and insist on accommodation. What makes you unhappy? What would it take to solve your problem? How can that be accomplished?
- Consider whether you contribute to your dissatisfaction. Identify the subtle forms of self-sabotage and eliminate them. For example, take control of your calendar and build in some "down time" instead of allowing your secretary to fill every moment with client meetings or court appearances.

- Learn to handle yourself personally in a manner that makes you comfortable in the face of conflict. Let go of the need to control every aspect of the client's problem. Half the fun of lawyering is the challenge of overcoming the obstacles that the client's situation presents. Accept this as a challenge in and of itself. Refuse to be part of the problem.
- Don't focus on your dissatisfaction or discuss it constantly. Focus instead on what you like about your practice. What's right with it? How can you get more of what you like?

CHAPTER 26

PERCEPTION IS REALITY

Recognize that management's perception of events, just because it is based on different and often superior knowledge, is not the same as the perception of other lawyers in the firm. Unless lawyers communicate with management regularly and openly, management has no way of knowing about the perception of certain events "in the trenches." Yet that knowledge is essential. The only way to get it is to seek the information.

Managers often take the position that they are "all knowing"—the most "in touch" with up-to-date information about the most important aspects of managing the firm. This is often far from the truth. Understand that the higher up the organizational ladder a manager is, the less those at lower levels will talk candidly with him. Most lawyers believe that senior management is out of touch with the problems and concerns of lawyers within the firm, and often it is. Lawyers and the managing partners of the firm become disconnected because both fail to talk openly and honestly together, lawyers don't trust management, and management is slow to resolve concerns. In large practices, management must make an effort to develop personal relationships with all lawyers to avoid isolation and misunderstandings.

Often we hear stories about the lawyer who is very respected within the firm, but doesn't know he is highly valued and leaves. A midlevel female lawyer left her firm because she wanted to have a child and didn't think the firm would accommodate a change in her schedule. This was her perception, although the managing partners believed the firm was accommodating to women and family issues. This lawyer's perception governed her reality, and changing her perception was necessary to keep her. Best Practices do a good job of informing lawyers about the firm's willingness to accommodate any lawyer who wants to combine a family with practicing law.

The family obligations of both male and female lawyers are becoming more significant and must be openly and candidly addressed. A junior partner, after the birth of her second child, told her firm she needed a part-time schedule. The senior partner in her practice group opposed the idea. He sincerely perceived that working part-time is "throwing her career away":

> *I know he has my best interests at heart. We've worked together a long time and he's always been my mentor. But he's put his career ahead of his family and he thinks that's the only way it can be done. I want to do other things in addition to practicing law.*

The senior partner in this scenario is convinced that the junior partner is wrong, and that her career will suffer if she works part-time. She hopes she can change his views before they must part company. To do so, she has begun talking with him regularly about her work, her successes, client satisfaction with her work, and her continuing efforts to build her practice. This will help the senior partner see that she is still a dedicated lawyer, but now has other obligations as well. Once again, honest communication is the key to changing perceptions.

An administrator of a medium-sized firm told us:

> *Our associates are passive-aggressive. They become unhappy and they just leave. If they're dissatisfied, it's their responsibility to say so and try to work it out.*

Although it may be the lawyer's responsibility to voice concerns, it is unrealistic to expect a junior lawyer to take charge in this way in an at-will employment atmosphere. Many up-and-coming lawyers are unwilling to be open and honest, for fear of losing of promotional opportunities or being viewed as a complainer. Remove this perception by open-door policies or forums that encourage communication. A well-regarded fifteen-year lawyer who has worked in private practice and as corporate counsel will likely leave the profession soon if her practice doesn't learn about her concerns:

> *I sometimes feel like someone with my personality (intellectual, somewhat introverted, consensus builder, not overly interested in power, prestige, or winning) has no place in the legal field.*

Provide effective mentoring so that the firm has a better idea of its lawyers' real needs. A junior partner told us about an associate he counseled:

> *He was a nice guy, from out of town, with no family here. I ran into him at a couple firm functions and we talked about the firm—what I liked about it, and why I came here from my last two jobs. I told him why I thought the firm was a good place for a junior lawyer. I didn't see him again for a while, but at Christmastime he brought a nice wine basket over to our house. I was really surprised. But he told me that he had been on the verge of accepting a job back in his hometown when he ran into me. He said the things I'd told him had really made a difference in how he felt about the firm and he had decided to stay.*

As firms get bigger and client demands grow, firms cannot count on such serendipity. Provide avenues for lawyers to share their concerns. If a lawyer works with only a few others within the firm, those few become the lawyer's view of the firm as a whole. If the lawyers with whom one works are not open to flexible schedules, for example, and are very demanding, one will come to believe that the firm's views are the same. Often it is those very partners who need retention assistance. Their departments have high attrition rates and management may not understand why.

Routinely evaluate the firm as a whole, as well as the various practice groups, to assess job satisfaction levels. Look at the ratio of male-to-female lawyers in the group, knowing an imbalance may signal a problem. Review the mix of junior lawyers to more senior lawyers, and minority lawyers to majority lawyers. Some commonality is often necessary for lawyers to communicate openly. The firm may need to provide mentors for lawyers outside their practice areas.

Most major businesses and at least two of the "Big 5" accounting firms have taken affirmative steps to advance women and minorities in business. Best Practices are doing the same. Most well-meaning majority male managers do not believe that their practices are unfair or unsupportive of women or minorities. Recognize that it is not the male managers' opinions that are important on the issue: it is the women and minority lawyers themselves who must believe the firm supports them. Recent research by the Massachusetts Institute of Technology revealed that women scientists on the faculty—even when there seemed to be no ill intentions—suffered from gender disparities in distribution of research grants, awards, appointments, and laboratory space, based on gender stereotyping. According to the research, such stereotyping marginalized the women, undervalued their achievements, and excluded them from positions of power. Corporate America, the Massachusetts Institute of Technology, the "Big 5" accounting firms, and Best Practices are working to change not only these results, but the thinking that produces them. Women lawyers believe that gender discrimination is pervasive and destructive, even when there is no blatant intimidation or harassment. Because women believe it to be so, practices must deal with the perception as if it were reality. The same is true for all forms of race discrimination.

Think creatively about what the firm needs to do to change perceptions. Understanding perceptions is just the first step. The firm must ascertain how the erroneous perceptions came to exist and what is necessary to change them. If lawyers have the perception, for example, that the firm will not accommodate a political campaign, it might be helpful for senior lawyers to speak to junior lawyers about how they previously managed political campaigns. If the lawyer's practice area is less accommodating than other areas of the firm, consider sharing more progressive practice group policies. Most practices quickly discover that anything they do to accommodate their lawyers on a temporary basis pays off in the long run. One national firm provides a database to its lawyers so they may easily contact those offices that may accommodate a job-share arrangement or part-time schedules.

If lawyers perceive a problem with retention, for example, management might look at the firm's numbers compared with the national and regional averages. If the practice doesn't have a high level of attrition, it can publicize that fact in newsletters and other forums. If it does, then management should explore the negative perceptions among its lawyers that are causing or contributing to the attrition—such as an incorrect perception that compensation is lower than other firms—and then take immediate steps to correct such perceptions.

The same is true for an analysis of billable hours. If the firm is perceived as a "sweatshop," is management satisfied with that perception? If not, how does the firm's billable-hour requirement compare with other firms? Is the requirement too high? If not, why do the lawyers feel the firm is a "sweatshop"? Is it because hours are constantly scrutinized or have recently been increased, or because lawyers don't get adequate credit for nonbilled time? Take steps to discover the problem and develop a plan to change perceptions by providing facts, asking for feedback, and responding promptly.

Any analysis of perception must start with fact gathering. Next, an open exchange must occur for the firm to discover how to deal with the problem. Then, the firm needs to publicize its point of view. Lawyers may simply not know what management is thinking and, therefore, make up their own erroneous version of events. Understand that although management may wholly disagree with lawyer perceptions, perceptions are the reality of those who perceive them, and they must be addressed accordingly.

BEST PRACTICE STRATEGIES

- Manage perceptions, just as other aspects of a successful practice are managed. Lack of information creates a vacuum into which many lawyers will insert negative beliefs. Assuming that "no news means good news" is rarely a good management strategy.
- When attempting to determine the best ways to communicate, consider the following criteria: (1) Does the message reach all lawyers throughout the organization? (2) Is the message clear, from both the firm and department level perspectives? (3) Does the media personalize the message for lawyers and show each lawyer what it means to him or her? (4) Does it promote interaction, such as talking, planning, and taking action?

BEST LAWYER STRATEGIES

- Understand that there are many sides to every issue. Explore your perceptions—are they fact or fiction?
- Be creative in your approach to your perceptions. Discuss them openly. Nothing will change unless you are open to the idea that it will.
- Understand that every individual is his own greatest asset, regardless of whether that individual practices law or engages in some other life pur-

suit. If you doubt it, have an economist value the loss of your life as if you were presenting a wrongful-death claim. The economic loss of one lawyer alone is millions of dollars.

- Respect others and yourself. Demand respect from others for yourself. But remember, a little humility doesn't hurt, either.
- Use goal-setting skills to determine the next stages of your development as a lawyer, as well as your ultimate vision for your law practice.
- Take jobs and clients that move you toward your goals and vision. Do not build a practice or a lifestyle you don't want, even if it means not being able to pay the rent. Allow your practice the time it needs to develop into what you want it to be.
- Recognize the value of the equity you have in your career. Consider having that equity valued by an economist if you cannot do it yourself. Think about what it would cost your family to replace you. At a minimum, this is your value. Don't sell yourself for less.

CHAPTER 27

BE PROACTIVE

It's not enough to know what lawyers want; Best Practices also do something about it. Use the information you gather to improve the practice.

For years, a law firm we know conducted ineffective exit interviews with lawyers and support staff. The interviews were informal and friendly. They focused on telling the departing person that the firm was sorry to lose him (whether it was true or not) and asking whether he wanted to offer suggestions about how the firm might improve any perceived imperfections for coworkers who remained. Although these interviews were routinely conducted and occasionally would yield candid comments from the departing lawyers, no action was ever taken by the firm based on the information obtained. As a result, the exit interview became a standing joke among people who remained with the firm. It was humorously suggested that the next person to leave should say in the exit interview that he would have stayed, had the firm built a swimming pool and bought all lawyers a German car or fur coat. In short, the process lost its credibility and quickly became an example of management's lack of candor.

Organizations that conduct client or employee surveys seeking suggested improvements face the same issue. When no changes are readily apparent to interested observers, asking the question without immediate reaction becomes worse than never asking at all. Instead, firms should ask for candid feedback and resolve the problems that are reported.

A related issue that arises frequently concerns communication of issues from the lower ranks to the higher ones, or what is termed "indirect communications." Ute Fisher, an adjunct assistant professor at Georgia Tech's School of Literature, Communication, and Culture, has studied commercial aircraft cockpit communications. She reported that many airplane crashes are forewarned by crew members in a tentative, suggestive way that is ignored or discounted by the pilot, with disastrous results. Her conclusions apply to environments where power, status, seniority, or age differences are prevalent, such as most law firms, departments, and agencies. The differences between airline cockpits and lawyer organizations are significant and variable, but the implication is clear: People struggle to get up the nerve to mention something casually and, once they do, management has a short window of opportunity to take it seriously and do something about it.

A four-year lawyer working in the corporate department of a large firm decided he wanted to join the probate department and make it his area of specialty. He talked with the head of the probate department and a senior associate, making his preference known. Both told him they'd be happy to have him join the department and would arrange to have his office moved. Four months later, the associate resigned to accept a job in the probate department of another firm, where he has since built a significant probate practice. When his firm expressed shock and surprise that he was leaving, he was amazed:

> I told them I wanted to change my specialty four months earlier. When I resigned, the managing partner told me they had been aware of my desire to do probate work and they were working on it. I was incredulous. I said I had waited four months for some sign that they would let me move into the department before I accepted another job, and he told me that four months wasn't very long in a forty-year legal career.

The most successful practices take hints, suggestions, humorous asides, and jokes seriously and act upon them promptly. An actual complaint is a rare thing to receive because no one wants to be perceived as negative or lacking dedication to the group or the practice. If one complaint is actually voiced, there are usually more that remain unspoken. Uncovering dissatisfaction and taking prompt remedial action are necessary.

In law firms in particular, there are usually no appropriate channels for lawyers to voice complaints or concerns. Corporations and agencies have human resource departments that act as shuttle diplomats between employees and management. Firms generally do not have anyone in such a role. If the recruiting and retention director has the authority to receive complaints from associates, there is no similar role for partners and shareholders. Adopt appropriate procedures to allow an independent party to receive comments and suggestions for improvement and change. A prompt response to every comment is imperative; the same day is not too soon to acknowledge receipt of the information. Not more than two weeks should go by without taking some further action, even if the further action is merely to explain that the problem cannot be immediately remedied.

Sensitive problems, such as inappropriate behavior by lawyers toward one another or staff, must be handled more carefully, but they must be handled. When the paralegals "jokingly" present one of the associates with "the lawyer most difficult to work for" award, that associate should be counseled on the proper working relationship between lawyers and support staff. When it becomes apparent that a supervising lawyer or department head is not promoting her subordinates or completing their reviews on time, then even if no formal complaint has been made, that situation must be addressed and the subordinates must be told it is being addressed—now.

When lawyers get the idea that behavior unacceptable to them is going to be accepted by the organization after the organization is aware of its existence, they will look for another place to work.

Focus groups, associate reviews, climate surveys, firm retreats, and partner or practice group meetings are also places where practices can seek comments, suggestions, and complaints, and award compliments. Most people feel they don't get enough honest recognition and they're right. At weekly practice group meetings, find ways to appreciate lawyers and give recognition. Report successes. Take the initiative to identify goals, aspirations, and areas needing improvement. If a team meeting is silent except for comments by the team leader and formal reports, the meeting is a failure because no real communicating is occurring.

Management should be vigilant about learning and exploring trends in the profession, staying aware of trends, and making conscious, consensus decisions about how to deal with them. Practices must be proactive, not reactive.

BEST PRACTICE STRATEGIES

- Appoint a senior and trusted lawyer to receive any concerns other lawyers may have. Make sure the appointee wants the job and the organization takes the appointment seriously by making the appointee's compensation and promotion dependent on how promptly and successfully concerns are resolved. Don't forget to ask colleagues to review the appointee's responsiveness and competence in resolving concerns.
- Adopt as a goal the "100-Percent Satisfaction Guaranteed" motto of certain retail establishments. Most people are satisfied with a response that says "it can't be done right now," if that response is true. However, when such a response is due to mere inflexibility or avoiding unpleasantness, it will be rejected.
- Continually remind all lawyers to be sensitive to the concerns of others, to suggestions they receive, and to "jokes" and comments made during social occasions. Everyone on the team is responsible to, and for, everyone else.

BEST LAWYER STRATEGIES

- State your concerns clearly to the appropriate person. The earlier a concern is stated and addressed, the easier it will be to make changes.
- Avoid hostile behavior. Practice your presentation skills by voicing your concerns in a positive way.
- Always consider and offer a solution to the problem you've identified. Request a response by a specified date. Follow up if the response is not forthcoming. In other words, treat your own concerns as if you were handling a client's concerns and expect the same results.

CHAPTER 28

APPLY THE PLATINUM RULE

Treat lawyers not just the way management believes is fair, but the way the lawyers themselves believe is fair. A satisfied lawyer will stay with the firm longer and lend her considerable talents to the firm for their mutual benefit.

We all remember the "Golden Rule" from our grade school training: Do unto others as you would have others do unto you. The "Platinum Rule" takes that concept one step further, recognizing differences in people and cultures: Do unto others as *they* would have you do.

We have heard some amazing stories of how lawyers behave toward one another, their colleagues, and their clients. One senior partner who is now deceased was reputed to throw books at his secretary when she would interrupt his train of thought. Another would banish his secretary to a different floor of the firm when she displeased him, after the screaming fight ended. Senior associates have received "awards" from their support staff for being the most difficult to work with. Lawyers test subordinates to see whether they can find existing law. Partners scream obscenities directly into the face of subordinates. Opposing counsel refuse to agree to any accommodation of any kind. In some cases, misrepresentations and outright lies are told to the court, in writing. "Rambo litigators" have inspired seminars and presentations aimed at how to avoid them and the tactics they employ in the name of "advocacy," following the precepts of *Winning by Intimidation* and *Business Secrets of Attila the Hun*. Senior lawyers dump work on junior lawyers' desks at 5:30 on Friday afternoon, ask for a return work product "first thing" on Monday morning, and then don't look at the work for weeks. Judges scream at lawyers, throw files, and storm off the bench. Other judges routinely keep lawyers and litigants waiting in their courtrooms while they attend to personal matters. Lawyers "joke" that the cost of litigation could be reduced significantly if they could avoid waiting time spent in court.

It goes without saying that all such abusive behaviors are unprofessional, unnecessary, and unacceptable, and should be obliterated. If there are members of your practice who participate in these forms of coworker abuse, you should take immediate steps to eliminate the offenses, even if it means eliminating the offender. This type of behavior reflects badly on the organization, the profession, and everyone in it. It will cause serious harm to the firm and the lawyers who practice there.

A junior partner with whom we spoke explained the abusive treatment of other lawyers in the firm this way: *"Abused children become abusive parents."* His point was that senior lawyers remember how they were treated and they treat others accordingly. Best Practices and Best Lawyers know the time to break that cycle is now.

A recently released study by the Gallup Poll, reported in *First, Break All The Rules: What The World's Greatest Managers Do Differently,* a book by Marcus Buckingham and Curt Coffman, which contains the results of two large studies conducted over twenty-five years by the Gallup organization, suggests that the one thing most employees want from their jobs more than anything else is a great boss. In this context, a great boss means an immediate supervisor who handles the needs of her employees. To the extent that you want to create loyalty in lawyers, train the supervisors.

The more subtle issue we want to address in this chapter, though, is when the firm and its partners are applying the Golden Rule, but the rules of the game have changed. Just because the firm's senior partners were hired into the firm at salaries below $10,000, and worked in an apprentice system for years before receiving significant compensation, does not mean that the firm's lawyers will do so in today's environment. Partnership buy-ins have been significant in the past, based on the equity the firm had created in its institutional clients, the capital equipment it owned, and so on. Today, many lawyers will not pay such sums without a significant reason to do so, generally defined as a guaranteed return on their equity investments. In years past, midlevel partners worked years to provide income for senior partners who had "earned it," and to pay out retirement income for those partners. Today, midlevel partners have not spent their entire careers with the firm, do not have the loyalty to senior partners their counterparts once had, and resent "paying for dead wood."

A midlevel partner with a portable specialty practice generating over a million dollars of annual revenue recently told us:

> *The senior partners in our firm are taking out way more than they're contributing. The way my practice is going, I could do significantly better if I opened my own shop. I'd like to stay here because there's some security in being with a firm, but I work too hard and I don't see my family enough to make what I'm taking out. What the senior guys are doing is really unconscionable and I know other partners who feel the same way.*

A senior partner, when approached with the suggestion that his contribution did not match his income, said:

I was underpaid the first ten years I worked for this firm and I intend to be overpaid the last ten years.

Understand that managing the firm the same way it's always been done is not sufficient in today's environment. The issue is not how senior lawyers were treated when they were in the positions that junior lawyers are now. The issue is how those junior lawyers want to be treated today. Learning the answer to that question—and providing the level of support lawyers currently want and can get elsewhere—is required.

Lawyers leave their current jobs for a variety of reasons, most of which are either a complete surprise or never learned by management. To ferret out what your lawyers want is the challenge of practice leaders. If you have developed a sufficient level of trust and support in your organization, the lawyers may very well tell you. They won't tell you repeatedly or forcefully, but they will advise you of their views. If you haven't developed that level of trust, they won't even gently suggest what they want.

Don't think mild levels of dissatisfaction reported to firm leaders are insufficient to cause lawyers to depart. One well-regarded and successful lawyer we know had been with her firm for over twelve years. She felt the firm was not properly valuing her contributions and told the executive committee so through formal review sessions. She also shared her views with individual executive committee members on informal occasions. When the changes she requested didn't happen, and when no member of the executive committee contacted her to explain why, she resigned. The interesting thing was the executive committee's reaction. They were shocked. They had no idea her concerns were deep enough or serious enough to cause her to leave the firm. Of course, management did not feel it was treating her unfairly. Both before and after she resigned, each manager told her that she was an integral part of the firm's future and a valuable member of the team. They said, "We knew you were unhappy, but we didn't think you'd leave." Her departure has cost the firm more than two million dollars a year. More important, as a respected lawyer within the firm, her departure caused other lawyers to question management, and other departures followed. Failing to apply the Platinum Rule caused a domino effect, from which the firm never recovered.

The point here is that well-trained, successful senior lawyers have a variety of options and can always negotiate better deals, if the firm is unwilling to accommodate them. We have been asked by senior management how to handle the situation when the lawyer makes "unreasonable" demands. The relevant inquiry here is, unreasonable to whom? Clearly, the demand is not unreasonable to the demanding lawyer; it is only perceived as unreasonable by management.

In these situations, we suggest the parties consider hiring an outside professional mediator to resolve the issue. What may work is an opportunity to air

opposing views with a trained facilitator who can assist the parties in fashion-
ing an acceptable compromise. In the absence of some innovative approach,
the practice should expect the lawyer to leave and make preparations to separate gracefully.

The Platinum Rule isn't as easy to apply as the Golden Rule because it
requires the practice to take proactive measures to figure out what lawyers want
and to satisfy those needs. Busy management teams would usually prefer the
tornado approach: Keep your head down and hope it passes over without too
much damage. By applying the Platinum Rule, practices can at least have some
input into the final decisions lawyers make. Seek that opportunity.

BEST PRACTICE STRATEGIES

- Pay attention to the kind of atmosphere you are creating in your organization and the behavior of all lawyers. Reward what you want, and
deal with what you don't want as soon as you learn of it. Don't expect
bad behavior to go away by itself.

- Engage partners with whom lawyers may talk freely about concerns,
and then correct any problems that arise.

- Reexamine compensation policies to be sure that seniority and past
performance are not overly weighted. Keeping new talent out of the
partnership because senior partners feel entitled to a larger share of
profits is shortsighted and denies the firm its future.

- Make sure everyone has the opportunity to advance based on objective
criteria that are controlled by the lawyer. Do not make the choice a
popularity contest or a political one.

- Consider dividing partnership into classes (such as "A," "B," and "C")
that require different levels of participation and provide different levels of reward. Let lawyers choose and accept the levels in which they
feel comfortable participating fully.

- Be sure lawyers know partner responsibilities and rewards. Some
lawyers won't want to be equity partners because the job is too
demanding and not sufficiently rewarding. Respect that choice and
make a place in the organization for those lawyers, too.

- Listen when your lawyers talk to you. Encourage open and honest
communication. Create an environment where open and honest communication without fear can exist.

- Act on what you learn. Either make the changes that are requested, or
explain in a truthful way why such changes can't be made. If the firm
is unwilling to accommodate the lawyer, expect the lawyer to leave in
search of what he feels he needs. Any good lawyer can argue both sides
of any issue. Do not leave these conversations believing you have per-
suaded the recalcitrant lawyer to accept your point of view.

BEST LAWYER STRATEGIES

- Ask your colleagues what they want. Don't assume you know. Just because you are willing to put up with it, or don't want to deal with it, don't assume others will feel the same.

- Define and be sure of your own goals. Do you really want to be a partner in this firm? Or would you be happier in another role? What would it be? Seek that role instead.

- Understand clearly the firm's requirements for advancement to the position you personally desire. Either meet those requirements, negotiate a change, or accept that you will not meet your goals. Restate your goal into one you can meet.

- Recognize that your future is completely under your control. Your income and advancement are not limited by anything other than your own thinking. Think big.

PART 3

SEPARATE GRACEFULLY

When separation is inevitable, separate gracefully. This is the time to create or solidify a marketing opportunity. Every lawyer has alumni potential. The relationship between the firm and every lawyer should last a lifetime.

So many lawyers have told us of unhappy and distasteful business divorces from prior partners and practices that are counterproductive, as well as expensive in the short run and for the long term, and that leave bitterness beyond reasonableness. Though there are similar stories in the business world, they are less prevalent and seem to be less venomous than legal world separations. This is another area where law practices and lawyers would do well to learn from the best practices of other businesses.

The practice of law as a group, even a group of two, is a voluntary association that can be terminated by either party at any time for any reason—a true at-will relationship, and at the same time a mutual-satisfaction contract. We are not suggesting that the voluntary nature of the relationship should be changed, and we find distasteful the suggestions we've heard related to tying lawyers together by financial commitments that will make it more difficult for them to leave if they choose to do so. What we advocate is a system that makes lawyers not *want* to leave a particular practice because they believe the practice is the best possible career choice for them at the present time.

We recognize, however, that disagreements will occur, desires will change, and lawyers—like other people in other lines of work—will want to move on to other projects, other work, and other practices. When that occurs, lawyers do themselves and their practices a disservice by parting angrily. Losing a long-held job is enough of an emotional roller coaster. Losing friendships fostered after years of working together is an unnecessarily harsh emotional price to pay for wanting to get involved in another position, for whatever reason. Beyond that, the continued business relationships that are often possible after parties separate are destroyed if lawyers and their practices fail to separate gracefully.

Recognize these truths and make it a goal to separate well from each other. This makes it easy to get back together in some way after the separation, either as partners again in the same association, or in mutually beneficial business or personal relationships. In Part Three we explore the most successful ways Best Practices and Best Lawyers separate gracefully, and the improved results that are possible by creating lifelong relationships that continue after separation.

CHAPTER 29

BEST PRACTICES
SEPARATE GRACEFULLY

Techniques exist for fostering cooperative, lucrative, and lasting business relationships with lawyers who leave your practice, regardless of the size of your organization.

Preparing to separate gracefully is counterintuitive to the concept of lawyer retention. Even after making lawyer retention a primary goal of the practice, a secondary goal should be the objective of creating a lifelong relationship with every lawyer who is added to the firm. Most lawyers and practices get new business from people who know them and have used them, either as clients or referral sources. The more clients and referral sources the business can maintain, the greater the likelihood of long-term success and survival of the practice. Best Practices understand this and make their internal customers—lawyers and support staff—sources of referrals and clients. It is inevitable that some attrition will occur, either at the request of the practice or at the behest of the lawyer. When that happens, despite the practice's best efforts to retain the lawyer, the second-best success is to maximize the alumni potential of every lawyer.

The worst possible alumnus is the disgruntled lawyer. Research has shown that 96 percent of clients won't tell the practice they're unhappy, but they'll tell others. The same general rule applies to disgruntled and disaffected lawyers. They can hurt the practice in ways that are exceedingly damaging—and the practice may not even be aware of it.

Assuming the departure of a friend of the firm, management should attempt to help the alumnus make the best placement. In general, the best placement—in descending order of desirability—is as follows:

- Potential client (assuming the alumnus will not replace the firm by taking the in-house position) or referral source
- Current client or referral source
- Law schools from which the practice recruits students
- Judicial offices
- Competitive firms

The major impediment to making sure no disgruntled lawyers leave the practice is the lack of a program to ensure job satisfaction for lawyers. Generally, lawyers do not give much notice to the practice when they leave. Once a lawyer gives notice, he has already accepted another position—he has reached a decision and made a commitment to leave. There isn't much that can be done to change that point of view, although practices should try to do so every time. The practice has failed to satisfy this lawyer to the extent that he has conducted a job hunt and accepted another position. Creating a "goodwill" departure at this stage is extremely difficult, but should be attempted. Consider the following steps:

(1) Assign and designate a particular senior lawyer in the practice to receive all resignations, in writing. If the departing lawyer delivers the resignation personally, the assigned lawyer should express immediate regret at the departure and invite the lawyer to change her mind. Ask the lawyer when she plans to leave and assure her that she can stay with the practice as long as she needs to do so to fit her personal plans. Tell her who she needs to see to complete the paperwork associated with her departure.

(2) Ask a senior lawyer who has been friendly with, and supportive of, the departing lawyer and who is *known* to be supportive of the practice to speak with the departing lawyer immediately upon receipt of the resignation. He should ask the departing lawyer to change her mind and stay with the firm, and should offer to repair the problem or perceived problem that is causing the departure, if possible.

(3) The senior lawyer must first apologize to the departing lawyer for any perceived or actual transgressions by the firm, and then directly promise the firm's future support and ask for the lawyer's future support. He should attempt to make and get a return commitment. Most lawyers will not go back on their word. They may not end up as goodwill ambassadors, but neither will they become terrorists where the practice's reputation is concerned.

(4) Make the first move by offering to assist the departing lawyer in any way possible. Be sure to follow through on any offers of assistance.

(5) Assign the trusted senior lawyer to follow up with the alumnus on a regular basis, scheduling lunches and phone calls to

continue the relationship. If old wounds are ever discussed, he should assure the lawyer that the firm is sorry for the transgressions and would handle the matter differently if given the opportunity to do so.

(6) Begin with properly conducted exit interviews. Develop a standard set of questions to ask in an exit interview, which are designed to gather the lawyer's perceptions about the firm, and assign a particular lawyer to conduct exit interviews within twenty-four hours of resignation. Exit interviews are conducted the very day of the resignation to capture, to the extent possible, the lawyer's true feelings. Promise confidentiality in exchange for candor. When negative perceptions are identified, assume others within the firm also hold those perceptions and address them promptly. Keep track of the responses and immediately address any concerns that are raised. Seek neutral, nonthreatening information such as:

- Were there any particular senior lawyers who were better at training than others?
- What were your best experiences here?
- What would you suggest that we do to improve?
- What could we do to encourage lawyers to let us know before they give up on us and start looking for another job?

(7) Consider your hiring needs and, if you still have the need for the lawyer's expertise, conduct a follow-up exit interview six months later. If the move has been to "browner grass," ask the lawyer to return.

The time to avoid a disgruntled departure is long before it happens. Have good retention programs in place. The senior lawyer assigned to accept resignations should be in charge of maximizing the alumni potential of a lawyer who is dissatisfied and wants to change his work environment. The senior lawyer should take a proactive approach to assisting the lawyer with his job search. An outplacement firm can be hired for this purpose or, if the firm is large enough, an administrative person within the firm can be assigned. Attempt to place lawyers in one of the best alumni positions and keep the lawyer at the practice until a good placement has been found. At that time, a senior lawyer *known* to be supportive of the practice should be assigned to maintain the relationship on a regular basis.

Satisfied alumni can be targets of marketing efforts and sources of business, from either their own employers or clients they won't service. These alumni should be on the firm's mailing list. They should be invited to client or prospective-client functions. They should be cultivated just as any other client would be cultivated.

A partner who decided to leave her practice attempted to separate gracefully. All went well until former clients started placing work with her instead of her prior firm:

In each case, I refused the work unless the former client volunteered that it was going to pull the work from the old firm whether I took it or not. I thought that if the work was leaving the old practice anyway, why shouldn't I take it? But my former practice never believed I hadn't "stolen" its clients. Even now, years later, the old firm attempts to sabotage me whenever it can. I refer work out regularly. But never to my prior firm.

Alumni efforts will fail miserably if the alumnus left with ill will. A former senior associate with a large national firm was invited to attend an alumni party. She told us:

A lot of the firm's former lawyers came and it was great to see everyone. But most of us now work for the firm's competitors. No one wanted to refer work back to the firm. We sat there and referred work to each other. It was the most productive marketing thing I've ever done, but it sure backfired on the firm. I doubt they'll do it again.

Evaluate business from alumni in the same manner as business from other sources. If after two years the alumnus has never referred any business to the firm and the firm believes that the alumnus could have done so, recognize that a problem exists and acknowledge it. At that time, the practice must make a decision about whether to confront the alumnus. A decision to confront the alumnus and seek an explanation should be made carefully. Sometimes, it is best to just let the matter drop, as long as the alumnus is not actively impeding the progress of the practice. But if the alumnus is hiring lawyers away from the practice and recommending that the practice not be used for legal work, the problem must be addressed.

The trusted senior lawyer should have a frank but nonthreatening conversation with the alumnus again. The point of this conversation is to declare a truce and peaceful coexistence. Both sides should understand that it is to one another's benefit to separate gracefully and simply agree to part company for now. Let the matter lie dormant for at least two more years and then reevaluate the situation. People change and time changes people. The alumnus might be salvaged yet.

BEST PRACTICE STRATEGIES

- Tell a lawyer who decides to leave that you will be sorry to see him go. Ask what you can do to make the transition go smoothly. Do it.
- Refer business to the departing lawyer. It may take several efforts and she may never refer anything back. Do it anyway. She won't disparage you if you are a referral source.
- Understand attrition in the practice thoroughly. Look for patterns and opportunities to eliminate it or to enhance alumni potential. For example, determine whether lawyers leave the firm voluntarily or were *literally* asked to leave (a lot of rationalizing goes on here if the firm wasn't totally happy with the departing lawyer); look at who is leaving (experience level, gender, or race, for example); study what exit interviews

and gossip reveal about the reasons for the departures; and analyze where the lawyers go (to competitive firms, agencies, departments, or home, for example).

- Terminate lawyers with care, based on individual performance. Voluntary reductions-in-force are always better than involuntary reductions, so consider offering "buyouts" instead of layoffs. Reduced compensation systems are preferable to across-the-board reductions in staff. Generous severance packages and rationales that are true, as well as fair, should be offered when involuntary terminations are necessary.

- Recognize that every lawyer is an asset, not a cost. When the firm eliminates a lawyer, or a lawyer leaves voluntarily, an income-producing asset is lost. Value and appreciate the firm's assets appropriately.

- Remember that every lawyer is building a law practice. Support lawyers in their efforts to gain independence with clients, to enhance their value to your firm and to themselves.

- Understand that clients cannot be "stolen" any more than spouses can be "stolen." Clients leave because they want to go. Focus your energies on making clients want to stay instead of attempting to battle with departing lawyers over client loyalty.

- Separate gracefully from every lawyer. Help each succeed. You'll feel better, if nothing else. Revenge is a destructive emotion. If you need further motivation, lawsuits are seldom filed when no economic damages are suffered.

CHAPTER 30

BEST LAWYERS SEPARATE GRACEFULLY

Techniques exist for maintaining a cooperative, lucrative, and lasting business relationship after you leave an organization with which you've previously practiced.

Before they enter law school, the happiest future lawyers are focusing on building their careers. Every person with whom one comes into contact is a potential client or referral source, and this is certainly true of every organization in which one is involved. Often lawyers make incorrect choices for their first law jobs. Good lawyers recognize that in addition to the psychological cost of carrying a grudge against former employers and colleagues, the career-building cost is too high. For that reason alone, they adopt the attitude that separation should be done as gracefully as possible.

The first rule of personal freedom as a Best Lawyer is to be financially secure, so that career decisions will not be based on financial need, but upon financial choice. When lawyers graduate from law school, they typically have significant debt loads to service. Living expenses, professional wardrobes, taxes, and other necessary costs reduce the gross salaries paid to new graduates much more quickly than most of them grasp. The sooner they understand the value of a financial safety net, the more likely they will demonstrate peace of mind and grace under the pressures of law practice. Begin now to formulate a financial "Plan B" if you don't have one. Figure out how to live for six months or longer with no income whatsoever. Some ways to have this level of security almost immediately are the following:

- Secure a credit card with a line of credit equal to at least six months of take-home pay. Don't use the card for anything except replacement of lost wages.

159

- If you have a home, obtain a home equity line of credit. Don't use the line except for replacement of lost wages.
- Buy sufficient disability insurance if your job doesn't provide it. If the practice does provide disability insurance, buy your own independent insurance as soon as you can afford to do so.

As lawyers mature in the practice, they have a tendency to live the "accumulation phase" of life in a manner that is well above their means. Doing this is a sure ticket to bondage. Successful lawyers make it a priority to begin saving money immediately upon receiving that very first paycheck. These first jobs probably pay more money than the lawyers have ever been paid. The happiest lawyers save at least 25 percent of pretax income until they have at least a year's living expenses in a tax-free money market mutual fund. They know a hefty savings account buys freedom.

Because they have no economic necessity to stay in their jobs and can easily find others in six months or a year (the period of living expenses they've saved), Best Lawyers' views of the practice will be different. They have chosen to work in this practice and can leave anytime without notice and without another job. That level of freedom is priceless and provides a psychological edge.

After reading this book, a practicing lawyer should come to the conclusion that one of the prime mistakes lawyers make is failing to recognize that their personal perceptions are not necessarily reality. Much of what a lawyer believes occurs in a practice is just not true. Thus, a lawyer does a disservice to herself and her practice to formulate negative opinions about the organization and fail to test or resolve them. Happy lawyers are proactive in attempting to resolve any perceived issues with the practice. For example, until they approach their firms and attempt to create economic solutions, such lawyers don't simply assume that because senior lawyers work long, hard hours, their firms would be unwilling to allow them to work part-time while they raise children.

Recognize the need to be very direct in approach. Often, because every communication is filtered by the receiver, the senior lawyer with whom you discuss relevant issues doesn't really hear what you're suggesting because you're attempting to be politically correct. If your view is that you will not work 2,000 billable hours a year after your child is born, say exactly that. Suggesting that 2,000 is a lot of time for a new mother to work, or using other euphemisms, is simply not sufficient to be sure that both parties have understood the issue. Before concluding that the senior lawyer "just doesn't get it," ask, "What is your understanding of my concern?" You might be surprised at the lack of communication between the two of you.

A lawyer who feels he is a good negotiator for his clients but not for himself should obtain assistance—from an appropriate administrator in the practice, a senior lawyer with whom he feels comfortable, or an outside agent such as a lawyer or consultant—to help him with his negotiation.

After exploring solutions to the issues that trouble you, and finding intransigent management or no common ground, you may well conclude that you must find a new job. Ideally, the practice is one that encourages separating gracefully, wants a lifelong relationship with you, and will help you find a position that will meet your needs while keeping you on the job until you find it. In that case, advise management that because it can't resolve your problem, you will accept its offer to help you find work elsewhere.

Many law firms are less than enlightened about lawyer departures and will punish lawyers who give sufficient notice of resignation. In such a practice, Best Lawyers are prepared to leave immediately after submitting notice. Thoroughly understand your ethical obligations to clients and the practice and follow those obligations scrupulously, but be packed and ready to go before you give your notice.

Regardless of the practice's degree of enlightenment, leave on good terms with as many people as possible. This is not the time to begin a crusade, although you should be honest if asked why you're leaving. It is possible to be honest without being offensive. If the practice wasn't willing to resolve your concerns when you raised them while you were still an active part of the organization, it's unlikely management will make any effort to resolve those concerns now that you've decided to leave.

Remain friendly with former colleagues. Most of them were not on the management team anyway, and had little—if any—control over the issues that caused you to leave the practice. Keep them on your mailing list, talk with them regularly, and, if you respect their legal talents, refer work to them when you have the opportunity to do so. Be friendly when you see them at professional or social gatherings. They are some of your best sources of future business and they have the ability to affect your personal and professional reputation, either positively or negatively. The legal world is a very small one. Never underestimate the opportunity for future contacts with former colleagues.

Remember that the former practice and former colleagues are concerned about your dissatisfaction reflecting negatively on them as well. Reassure them whenever you have the chance to do so.

A former lawyer's aura of expertise is related to the training and opportunity he received from every practice with which he has been associated. That aura will be tarnished if he tarnishes the aura of the former practice. As far as the world is concerned, it's much better to advise all inquirers that he left the former practice for a "better opportunity." Surely there are objective facts to support this view, even when being asked by a close friend or potential employee of the former practice.

Even if the lawyer has been asked to leave the practice, both parties should still separate gracefully. Sharing bitterness and resentment with prospective clients and colleagues does no one a service. Everyone understands that if the relationship had been perfect, the two of you would still be together. The details of the separation are best kept private.

BEST LAWYER STRATEGIES

- Become an "A player," or a high value added/hard to replace Best Lawyer. If you are, you can make your living anywhere and any organization will want you.
- If you conclude that you must leave, depart on fair terms. Talk with the firm about how your future goals might connect with the goals of the firm, and be open to a mutually satisfactory relationship in the future.
- Remember that a referral base for lawyers is essential to a healthy practice. Keep in touch with former colleagues and refer work to the ones with whom you have established relationships. A legal career is based on relationships and networking. Keep your network even if you leave your job.
- Separate gracefully from your practice, if possible. But do not lie when you leave. If you are dissatisfied with the practice, say so in a nonaggressive way, without hostility, so the relationship can continue.
- Don't talk with others about the reason for your separation. The reason you left your former practice was for a "better opportunity." Stick to your guns on this one. If you remain above the fray, your former practice can find no fault with your behavior.
- Accept any help your former firm wants to give you. You incur no obligation by doing so.

CONCLUSION

Although this is the conclusion to our book, we don't believe our work will ever be concluded. Humans will always seek happiness and lawyers will always be human. At a certain level of human development, and in American culture that seems to be somewhere in midlife, we all seek more meaning in our lives. We get the message that life is short and, reincarnation theories aside, this is likely the only chance we get to do it right. When that happens, we look more closely at our personal and professional lives and refuse to accept that "that's all there is."

In the context of lawyering—regardless of whether you are less optimistic or tend toward workaholism, or have been so well trained in the law that you always see the risks as outweighing the benefits of any activity—the very real pressures of the economics of law practice will inevitably result in searching for something more. This is true even if you are supremely successful and satisfied with the work. Satisfied lawyers are so because they have found meaning in their work, have developed control over their practices, have respect for themselves and their clients and receive respect in return, have made peace with their financial lives, and have lives outside the law practice.

The message we've sought to convey is that this search is a normal part of a lawyer's development today; job satisfaction is possible at every level of practice and lawyer retention is a direct result of job satisfaction. Job satisfaction for lawyers is not a matter of leaving the lawyer alone to figure it out. Some lawyers do successfully resolve the issues for themselves, but far more either keep searching without finding what they want or give up. We believe that law is a calling—a vocation—and has the potential to be so flexible that there is no reason to be unhappy or to resign. We hope this book has convinced you as well that "Happy Lawyer" is not an oxymoron.

SAMPLE ASSOCIATE DEVELOPMENT PLAN©

GOAL: To gain consensus, and to reduce to writing and promulgate career benchmarks for associates from entry level to partner (and beyond). Commit to advancing lawyers who fulfill their benchmarks and refusing to advance lawyers who do not.

HOW:
1. Design time lines for responsibility and development.
2. Give supervisory lawyers guidelines for delegation of work and evaluation of junior lawyers.
3. Encourage delegation so lawyers at each level have challenging work; reward low cost and efficiency instead of raw billable hours.
4. Emphasize teamwork, organization, communication, and other management skills.
5. Base compensation on achieving firm objectives as well as individual objectives.
6. Make the process as simple as possible, to encourage continuing participation.

EXAMPLE:
1. In the first year following law school, associates will:
   (a) Determine and develop a personal career plan
   (b) Take at least [number] depositions
   (c) Write at least [number] substantive briefs that will be filed essentially unchanged with the court (or draft other types of simple documents effectively)
   (d) Attend at least [number] client conferences

    (e) Master billing guidelines and reporting time

    (f) Master supervisory techniques for dealing with support staff effectively

    (g) Attend hearings, client meetings, and counsel conferences as "nonbillable" learning experiences

    (h) Actively participate on [number] internal committees

    (i) Join [number] sections of bar associations

    (j) Prepare a personal marketing plan that includes generating a personal mailing list

    (k) Complete a self-evaluation that demonstrates awareness and understanding of goals and performance

2. In the second year following law school, associates will:

    (a) Review and revise personal career plan and adjust annual goals accordingly

    (b) Take more difficult depositions, attend hearings alone, and conduct simple client and counsel meetings

    (c) Prepare more difficult and more substantive briefs or documents, with cursory review by senior lawyers

    (d) Actively participate on internal committees and chair one committee

    (e) Assist with career development of more junior lawyers, including summer associates

    (f) Consider senior lawyers and determine who would make an effective mentor

    (g) Accept a lead assignment from at least one bar association committee

    (h) Revise personal marketing plan and begin rainmaking training

    (i) Complete a self-evaluation that demonstrates awareness and understanding of goals and performance

3. In the third year following law school, associates will:

    (a) Review and revise personal career plan and adjust annual goals accordingly

    (b) Accept personal responsibility for development of career from this point forward

    (c) Accept first-chair responsibility for less sophisticated matters

    (d) Prepare more difficult and more substantive briefs or documents, with cursory review by senior lawyers

    (e) Delegate to—and review work of—junior lawyers and paralegals

    (f) Actively participate on internal committees and chair a different committee with greater firm management responsibilities

(g) Assist with career development of more junior lawyers, including summer associates

(h) Work with a senior lawyer mentor effectively

(i) Become an officer of at least one bar association committee

(j) Revise personal marketing plan and accept responsibility for appropriate use of a rainmaking budget

(k) Complete a self-evaluation that demonstrates awareness and understanding of goals and performance

4. In the forth and subsequent years following law school and later, lawyers will:

(a) Review and revise personal career plan and adjust annual goals accordingly

(b) Accept personal responsibility for development of career

(c) Accept first-chair responsibility

(d) Prepare substantive briefs or documents with cursory (if any) review by senior lawyers

(e) Effectively delegate to—and review work of—junior lawyers and paralegals

(f) Actively participate on internal committees and chair committees with greater firm management responsibilities

(g) Assist with career development of more junior lawyers, including summer associates, as an effective mentor

(h) Work with a senior lawyer mentor effectively

(i) Become a senior officer of at least one bar association committee

(j) Revise personal marketing plan and accept responsibility for appropriate use of a rainmaking budget

(k) Generate new clients and new business from existing clients

(l) Complete a self-evaluation that demonstrates awareness and understanding of goals and performance

APPENDIX B

DRAFTING AN EFFECTIVE MISSION STATEMENT[1]

A mission statement must be inspirational, motivational, evolutionary, and revolutionary. It should excite and energize, be concise and clear, and be simple to understand and remember.

Spend no more than half an hour discovering and writing your mission statement. This is a right-brain activity and needs to be more intuitive than logical. Once you write the mission statement, don't change it for at least six months. You must try it for a while to see whether your intuition has served you well. Following is a three-part process to writing a mission statement that you can "grow into":

Part One: Every mission requires action, and action requires verbs. Choose your three most meaningful, purposeful, and exciting verbs.

Part Two: What do you stand for? To what principle, cause, value, or purpose would you be willing to devote your life?

Part Three: Whom are you here to help? Every mission implies that someone will be helped. The more specific you can be, the more focused and powerful will be your energy. Pick only one group, entity, or cause you most would like to help or affect in a positive way if you can.

Your mission statement will then be Part One + Part Two + Part Three. Revise the language until you like the way it reads, and then leave it alone.

---

[1]This process is adapted for lawyers from the excellent book by Laurie Beth Jones, *The Path*, which is listed in our bibliography. Read Laurie's book for further explanation of her methods.

PART ONE: EXAMPLE VERBS

Quickly circle three verbs from each of the following seven lists. Then narrow that to the three that most excite you.

A.	B.	C.	D.
accomplish	compliment	embrace	heal
acquire	compose	encourage	hold
adopt	conceive	endow	host
advance	confirm	engage	identify
affect	connect	engineer	illuminate
affirm	consider	enhance	implement
alleviate	construct	enlighten	improve
amplify	contact	enlist	improvise
appreciate	continue	enliven	inspire
ascend	counsel	entertain	integrate
associate	create	enthuse	involve
believe	decide	evaluate	keep
bestow	defend	excite	know
brighten	delight	explore	labor
build	deliver	express	launch
call	demonstrate	extend	lead
cause	devise	facilitate	light
choose	direct	finance	live
claim	discover	forgive	love
collect	discuss	foster	make
combine	draft	franchise	manifest
command	dream	further	master
communicate	drive	gather	mature
compel	educate	generate	measure
compete	elect	give	mediate
complete		grant	model

E.	F.	G.
mold	reduce	support
motivate	refine	surrender
move	reflect	sustain
negotiate	reform	take
nurture	regard	tap
open	relate	team
organize	relax	touch
participate	release	trade
pass	rely	translate

perform	remember	travel
persuade	renew	understand
play	resonate	use
possess	respect	validate
practice	restore	value
praise	return	venture
prepare	revise	verbalize
present	sacrifice	volunteer
produce	safeguard	work
progress	satisfy	worship
promise	save	write
promote	sell	yield
provide	serve	
pursue	share	
realize	speak	
receive	stand	
reclaim	summon	

PART TWO: EXAMPLE VALUES

accountability	fairness	integrity
authenticity	faith	joy
beauty	family	justice
comfort	freedom	loyalty
competitiveness	fun	openness
cooperation	growth	peace
courage	happiness	service
creativity	health	spirituality
equality	honesty	trust
excellence	independence	

PART THREE: EXAMPLE GROUPS OR CAUSES

Below is a list of groups and/or causes. Pick the three that most attract you. Then select one for now. You may expand later, if you wish.

administration	construction	immigration	public safety
agriculture	defense	infants	real estate
animal care	design	journalism	religion
animal protection	education	justice system	reproduction

animal rights	elderly	labor	research
art	energy	labor relations	roads/bridges
biotech	environment	literacy	sexuality
books	family	management	space
border issues	fashion	media	sports
broadcasting	finance	movies	substance abuse
business	food	music	synagogues
child care	gardening	news	tourism
child protection	government	nonprofit agencies	travel
children	healthcare	nutrition	veterans
churches	home healthcare	parks/ recreation	water rights
civil rights	homelessness	politics	women's issues
community development	human development	poverty	youth
computer technology	illness and disabilities	printing/ publishing	

Part One: Write your three most exciting verbs here: _____, _____, _____.

Part Two: Write your values here: _____.

Part Three: Write your group or cause here: _____.

My mission is to _____, _____, _____ and _____ [to, for, or with] _____.

Revise the words until you like the way they sound and they form a mission statement you can get excited about pursuing. Then, rewrite your mission on an index card. Carry it with you for six months. Read it every two or three days. See how you feel about it. Do you like it? Does it fit you? How has discovering your mission affected your life? If you find the mission you've drafted doesn't suit you at any time after the first six months, then revise it to suit your present needs.

APPENDIX C

VISION MAPPING[1]

A vision statement is the end result of what you will have done. It is your ideal. The very moment you realize you are unhappy or frustrated with a situation is your point of power, for now you have a clear picture of how you don't want things to be. Imagine the exact opposite of the frustrating situation and there you have the makings of your vision. Focus on the life you want, and go after what you want directly.

The key elements of a compelling vision statement are these:

- It is written.
- It is written in the present tense, as if it has already been accomplished.
- It covers a variety of activities and time frames.
- It is filled with descriptive details that anchor it to reality.

Write your vision statement, incorporating your responses from these questions:

1. Who is living the life you most envy?
2. Describe what you think it is like.
3. Who is doing the kind of work you most wish you could be doing?
4. Describe what her work life must be like.
5. Who is the most successful lawyer you know personally? What characteristics does this person have that you believe mark "success?" How did she get to be so successful? Are you willing to do the same things—to "model" this person? Why or why

[1]This process is adapted for lawyers from several sources, all of which are listed in our bibliography.

not? How would you like your life to be different from hers? How can you accomplish that?

6. If you had only six healthy months left to live, what would they look like?

7. What do you want more of:
   - in your relationships?
   - in your work?

8. What do you want less of:
   - in your relationships?
   - in your work?

9. Describe in detail your ideal work setting.

10. Describe in detail your ideal workday.

11. Describe in detail your ideal coworkers.

12. Describe in detail your ideal client.

13. What kind of work would you do even if you didn't get paid for it?

14. If money were no object, what would you be doing with your life?

15. What would you do if you were ten times bolder:
    - in your primary love relationship?
    - in your work setting?
    - in your community?
    - in your family?
    - in your place of worship?

16. At work, what kinds of results are most meaningful to you?

17. What skills do you most enjoy using?

18. What kind of role do you enjoy most:
    - leader?
    - independent contributor?
    - expert?
    - manager?

19. What tasks and rewards motivate your best performance?

20. What kinds of clients do you want?

21. With whom do you want to work?

22. What would you have to do to live up to your potential?

23. Are you making a contribution? Is it the contribution you want to make?

24. How can you bring more artistry to your work?

25. In the last two or three assignments in which you were fully engaged, which three things were great about the work?

26. In the last two or three assignments in which you were not fully engaged, which three things made you dissatisfied with the work?

27. The last time you had fun at work, you were _____.

28. Imagine that it is 9:00 Monday morning, three years from now:
    - Where are you?
    - What are you doing?
    - Whom are you seeing?
    - What are you wearing?
29. It is now noon, same day:
    - Whom are you going to see?
    - Where are you going for lunch?
30. It is now 6:00 Saturday evening:
    - Where are you?
    - What are you doing?
    - Whom are you seeing?
    - What are you wearing?
31. What three things do you like best about your current practice?
32. Name three of your accomplishments that most amaze others.
33. If you had all the money you needed, how would you change your work life? Would you still practice law? Would you practice law the way you do now? Would you work as many hours? How many hours would you work? What would you do with the rest of your time?
34. Do you generally prefer to work longer hours because it increases your income?
35. Did you bill your expected number of hours last year? More? Less? If more, what did you get for it in the way of reward? If less, what disincentives were applied? Do you care? Is it your goal to bill hours, or to make $X? Or to get promoted? Or some other intangible goal? What would happen if you met that goal? What if you didn't?
36. You are now a very old person, walking with a child who asks you, "What are you most proud of about your life?" What do you say?
37. You are about to die. What did you accomplish before you left?
38. As a result of your having lived, three things have changed or shifted in the world. What are they?

Write your vision here:

APPENDIX D

CLEARLY DEFINING A SUCCESSFUL PLAN[1]

A successful plan requires clearly defined long-term and short-term goals that excite you and engage your interest. Identify broad strategies and narrow tactics to move toward each goal. Prioritized daily work will keep you on track and provide optimal experience every day.

GOALS

Goals are just an excuse to play the game; they are dreams with deadlines. Ask yourself these questions to determine yours:

- If I was *certain* of success, what would my heart-stopping dream be, as it relates to my work?
- Regardless of what I believe is possible, how many *paths* are there to this goal that I can think of right now? (Consider asking colleagues to join a brainstorming session to help identify potential paths that don't occur to you.)
- Which *one path* will I start, knowing my direction might change?

---

[1]This process is adapted for lawyers from several sources, all of which are listed in our bibliography.

STRATEGIES AND TACTICS

You must identify strategies and tactics. *Strategies* are broad plans; *tactics* are the "who, what, when, and how" to achieve each strategy:

- What *four strategies* will help me get to my vision?
- For each of my strategies, what are the important *tactics:* Who? What? When? How?

OBSTACLES AND SUPPORT

You must also identify *obstacles* (what is likely to get in your way) and *support* (who or what you can count on to help you) for each strategy or tactic:

- What *obstacles* do I foresee and how will I overcome them?
- What *support* from what people do I foresee I will need, and how will I ask for it?

REGULAR TASKS

Regular tasks are the monthly, weekly, and daily opportunities to choose and create flow activities that will provide you with a satisfying job every day. What will you do today? Make a list. You must choose tasks that challenge you, but that don't so far exceed your skill levels that you feel overwhelmed.

For example, attempting to write this book in one week would have been an overwhelming task. Setting such a goal would have been more stressful than fun. The goal would not have been achieved and we would have been "failures."

We made the project energizing and fun by breaking it down in various ways. First, we prepared the proposal and the table of contents. We enjoyed the project of identifying what we would do, how we would do it, what subjects we would cover, and so on. We discussed these topics over dinner, during shopping excursions, while drinking coffee or wine, while vacationing in Key West, and during weekends in Chicago and Palm Beach. We made the project fun and enjoyable so we would want to focus on it every day. When we submitted the proposal and table of contents, we celebrated!

Next, we divided the chapters between us and began research for each one. We gave ourselves some realistic deadlines for completing the initial drafts of the chapters. We struggled with the best method for getting our original ideas on paper, and then for doing the interviews and the research. By trial and error, we eventually settled on an approach that worked well. We used technology to allow us to work in many different locations. When we took plane trips, we carried along copies of the drafts for revision. We used e-mail and modem capabilities to communicate.

We looked for opportunities every day to discuss the project with other lawyers and gather the interview information we presented. We scheduled focus groups and individual interviews. We took lawyers to lunch, shared drinks, talked during work-related projects, and generally divided the research task into manageable bites.

Doing the reading, and researching management techniques and successful Best Practices and Best Lawyer techniques, was easier to do individually than together. We kept track of our research independently, but shared the information through regular weekly conference calls. Discussing our progress regularly was the most pleasurable aspect of this project.

The day we put the book together into a cohesive whole for the first time was another occasion for celebration. We like celebrations and engage in them often! Why not?

Then, we began to break down the revision task. We wrote the introductions, transitions, and conclusion. We read the book from cover to cover and revised accordingly. After revisions on the hard copy, computer work was next. Every day we would list three or four projects to be done that day. We'd check them off with glee and quit for now with great fanfare. Finally, we completed the work and submitted it. We bought ourselves a present to commemorate the occasion. The entire project took about a year of actual work.

In formulating your own daily tasks, use the flow model from Chapter 10. Remember to choose work that interests you, schedule tasks appropriately (without overcommitting), and celebrate each completion as a victory. Each day,

- Do something fun
- Find five things to be grateful for
- Take care of your body
- Take care of your family
- Do meaningful work
- Spend at least 30 minutes in solitude and reflection

Remember that like electricity, ambition can be life enhancing or destrucive. Pace yourself.

APPENDIX E

MORE STRATEGIES

MORE BEST PRACTICE STRATEGIES

- Understand from the outset what law practices are and what they sell: lawyers. Treat those lawyers as your most precious asset. Respect lawyers and their skills, talents, and contributions. A simple acknowledgment of the value of lawyers to the practice, the profession, and society would go a long way toward curing most lawyers' ills.

- Make an effort to calculate the value of the practice's intellectual capital. The result may surprise you.

- Identify high value added/hard to replace, "A player" lawyers and make sure they're getting what they need in your organization. Be flexible to keep them onboard. By definition, each lawyer adds to the firm's expertise, revenue, and reputation.

- Devote substantial resources to training and supporting every lawyer on your team. Teach each how to do the client development and legal work you desire. The "sink or swim" method may work for swimming lessons (though most of the time, they don't put you in deep water on your first day), but for building a successful law practice it is less than optimum.

- Decide what successful performance is, and then reward it promptly and often. Celebrate what's right.

- Recognize, acknowledge, and respect that law is a vocation. Address the economics of law practice in a manner that supports the goals of law as a vocation.

- Adopt your jurisdiction's ethics rules and oath of office seriously in your practice. Pay more than lip service to the idea that ethics rules are aspirational and that appropriate professional behavior is not inapposite to "advocacy." Lead by example.

- Nurture junior lawyers in professional and ethical behavior. Encourage and reward appropriate behavior and refuse to accept inappropriate behavior. Provide training in management and "people skills." Promote only those lawyers who conform to civility and professionalism in the office.

- Consider the public perception of lawyers and do your part to improve it. When you do good things for your community, publicize it—not just in the legal community, but in public service announcements in your local newspapers and on your local television stations. Seek to inspire trust in the community you serve.

- Get to know your lawyers. Only by understanding what they want can you fashion programs and plans that will keep them engaged. Invest in the group's lawyers and their personal lives. Develop personal relationships with them. Lawyers will stay with the practice if they like the people and enjoy working with one another.

- Consider paying lawyers retention bonuses after a certain number of years with the practice. Pay the bonus after the lawyer becomes most profitable and when the firm most needs him to stay. Paying the bonus in annual installments over two or three years may increase retention if the bonus is large enough.

- Keep track of what competitors in business are offering lawyers in your market, and either match the competition or compensate for failing to meet it with flexibility, camaraderie, opportunities, and other attributes of a great place to work.

- Recognize that long careers require constant tending, just like long-term marriages and other relationships.

- Identify what is important to each lawyer. Lawyers' needs will not differ all that much. Develop a flexible approach to the practice of law, so lawyers do not sense that the only way to improve their lives is to leave.

- Open the lines of communication. Talk with the lawyers themselves about their dissatisfactions to enable the practice to address those concerns.

- Help every lawyer in the practice create a great job—one that ensures happiness, productivity, and profitability. Commit to lawyer retention and improving job satisfaction for lawyers at every level of the practice.

- Commit to a lifelong relationship with every lawyer who enters the practice, even if at some time the lawyer separates from the practice. Make it easy for the lawyer to return.

- Offer training in conflict resolution, particularly for newer lawyers. Interpersonal relationships between opposing counsel should be professional and civil. A senior lawyer should step in when junior lawyers are being abused by either opposing counsel or other lawyers in the practice.

- Recognize that groups of lawyers view the practice differently. Men/women, junior associates/senior associates, associates/partners, minority/majority lawyers—all bring different expectations and perspectives to the practice. Create an environment free of overt or subtle bias by understanding these differences and celebrating them.

- Never reject a serious request by a lawyer for more flexibility, challenge, support, compensation, or anything else. Supporting the individual lawyer will most often benefit the practice, not cause serious harm. If you don't give lawyers what they want, they will seek it elsewhere.

- Constantly reevaluate the lawyers' needs, and recognize and deal with dissatisfaction immediately. Consider climate surveys to determine how the practice's lawyers feel now.

- Neither encourage nor accept lack of civility or professionalism from lawyers in the practice, regardless of their level of expertise. This behavior is truly harmful to the practice and the profession. Best Practices should do all within their power to eradicate it.

- Have each lawyer write a personal mission statement that interrelates to the organization's mission. Helping the organization succeed in its mission must be part of the firm's evaluation process for every lawyer.

- Assess culture from all angles. Only with a full understanding of the firm's culture will the firm be able to affect its environment positively. The firm must know the answers to these questions: "Who are we?" "What is the underlying atmosphere in the firm?"

- If the firm's culture has affected its lawyers negatively in the past, take affirmative steps to change it in a way that has a positive influence. Create an atmosphere that is completely free of both overt and subtle bias. A collegial atmosphere that is neither overly formal nor informal is preferred by most lawyers. Adopt casual dress codes. Encourage the use of first names. Respect everyone's time and talent.

- Reinforce the organization's desired culture with everything it does. Whether through recruiting, marketing, or day-to-day communication with clients, use every opportunity to reinforce a positive culture. For example, adopt positions such as these: "We don't take advantage of other lawyer's mistakes here." "We always do the ethical thing." "We treat one another with respect, from the mail room staff to the managing partner."

MORE BEST LAWYER STRATEGIES

- Recognize, acknowledge, and respect that law is a vocation.
- Negotiate for what you want. Don't just assume that your current firm won't match your best offer elsewhere. These days, many practices understand your options.

- Hire an agent. If you can't negotiate for yourself, hire someone to negotiate for you or to help you analyze and present your alternatives. The best choice is a consultant who knows your market, has no stake in your career, and can be objective. The second-best choice is a good, like-minded business lawyer who knows you, your strengths, and your skills well.

- Explore your options; know your market. You may think the grass will be greener elsewhere, and it may very well be so. But be sure before you leave one bad situation for another. Recognize that long careers require constant tending, just like long-term marriages and other relationships.

- Manage your finances to maximize your options. You should be saving at least 25 percent of your gross income. If you are, then you'll be living well below your means, you'll be able to weather a long period of unemployment or underemployment, and you will not feel trapped in a no-win situation. The psychological lift you get from this strategy alone will change your outlook and give you the strength to act in your best interests instead of from economic insecurity.

- Evaluate why you are dissatisfied. The first step to addressing your dissatisfactions is knowing what they really are.

- Recognize that job satisfaction is attainable and within your control. Just as changing spouses is no guarantee of a happy second or third marriage, changing jobs is no guarantee of job satisfaction. There are good reasons to move from one job to another (such as a desire to move to a new practice area that your current practice declines to develop after you've asked them to do so), but most job hopping is destined to fail because the job isn't the problem.

- Identify your goals and aspirations very specifically. Are they realistic? If you're stumbling while trying to achieve your goals, reevaluate. Move toward your dreams, not away from your nightmares.

- Respect and value your talent and your time. Do not sell yourself as a commodity to those who would demean what you do and who you are.

- Detach yourself from your client's cause. The old adage that "a lawyer who represents herself has a fool for a client" applies equally well to a lawyer who becomes his client by too closely identifying with his client's cause. This means not accepting contingent-fee work unless you can truly afford to work for free. Tying your own economic security to your clients' financial success *by definition* destroys your independence.

- Never engage in unethical, unprofessional, or uncivil conduct under any circumstances. Report any such activities by opposing counsel to appropriate regulators promptly. Do not be part of the public's poor perception of lawyers. Walk your talk.

- Determine your values and whether your goals mesh with the firm's overall culture. Openly communicate your beliefs about how the firm's culture affects your goals and aspirations. Be sure you understand the firm's view.

- Take every opportunity to carry the message of the firm's culture to others. If you have something nice to say, say it! If you have something negative to say, deliver it to appropriate people through appropriate channels instead of grousing to your friends at lunch.
- Recognize your value to your organization, without overvaluing or undervaluing yourself. Be sure your compensation adequately reflects your value. If you are undervalued, negotiate for a greater share of compensation. If you are overvalued, recognize that fact and work to improve your value. Recognize that your value is directly attributable to the amount of money you generate for your firm. Know what that is. Strive to improve it. You are your greatest asset. Make the most of your talents, abilities, and future.

APPENDIX F

HOW TO BE A HAPPY LAWYER©

Decide to be happy no matter what.
Be grateful for what you have.
Work less and accept the benefits of more time.
Know that billionaires are no happier than you.
Expect the best.
Work toward a positive outcome.
Follow the Platinum Rule: Treat others as they want to be treated.

Never complain.
Give up control.
Be reasonable.
Accept gifts graciously.
Tend clients carefully.
Be honest, neither pessimistic nor overselling.

Serve others.
Recognize that you attract clients, money, and success, not acquire them.
Remember that life is short.
Decide to be happy no matter what.

M. Diane Vogt

AFTERWORD

This work is not intended to be a statistical study or the definitive word on lawyer retention or improving job satisfaction for lawyers. What we hope we have accomplished is sharing our work with you in pursuit of our mission: "To encourage, facilitate, and promote the profession by improving job satisfaction for lawyers and keeping experienced lawyers available to the public."

We have told you what our colleagues have told us—information they may or may not have shared with you as well. We've done this in the hope that the profession, law practices, and individual lawyers will find the information useful in improving lawyer retention and job satisfaction for lawyers. We thank you for helping us toward our vision: "Lawyers we've counseled are happy people, well-satisfied professionals, respected by society, and leaders in their communities."

ABOUT THE AUTHORS

PeopleWealth provides retention consulting to law practices and individuals. PeopleWealth's retention consulting for organizations, Career Design process, and Career Building Coaching for individuals are designed to assist lawyers and practices in developing satisfaction, retention, and career plans that will meet the individual needs of lawyers and make them successful in their existing environments. Our mission is to encourage, facilitate, and promote the profession by improving job satisfaction for lawyers and keeping experienced lawyers available to the public. We do this through public speaking, consulting with law firms and individuals, conducting workshops, and writing for various publications. At our seminars—designed to provide techniques to improve job satisfaction, life balance, and quality of professional life—we are repeatedly gratified by our colleagues' intense interest in this subject and their desire to achieve job satisfaction. The desire to change is always the first step toward any new thinking. Our presentations often include information on the state of the profession, the cost to firms and lawyers of high voluntary turnover rates among lawyers, and suggestions for change. Our workshops promote personal responsibility for individual job satisfaction. What we know is that the profession cannot sustain itself on the concept of duty. Joy must be at least one goal.

PeopleWealth's principals are **M. Diane Vogt** (Michigan 1980; Florida 1989) and **Lori-Ann Rickard** (Michigan 1986; Florida 1998). Both women graduated cum laude from Wayne State University Law School and served on the Law Review. They were associates and partners in a large law firm in Detroit where they practiced together for several years. While they were with Clark, Klein & Beaumont (now, Clark Hill), they served as mentors and members of the training, recruiting, and marketing committees, in addition to keeping track of busy litigation practices and bar activities. Diane was an active member of the Michigan Bar Client Development and Law Firm Marketing Committee.

Diane moved her practice to Florida in 1992, where she built a firm that grew from four to nine lawyers and from two to eight paralegals. She started a second boutique litigation practice in 1995, using the innovative staffing techniques we recommend, such as contract lawyers, flextime, remote telecommuting, scheduling techniques, revenue sharing, and fee setting. Diane has been "AV" rated by *Martindale-Hubbell* in Detroit and Tampa since 1990 and 1994, respectively, and was selected by her peers as one of five defense lawyers in Florida they would recommend to clients with the need for a product liability defense lawyer. Diane has practiced law continuously for twenty years. She also taught law school courses for six years, as an adjunct professor at Wayne Law School from 1987 to 1991, and as a visiting teacher at University of South Florida. She is listed in *Who's Who* and *Who's Who in American Law*. Diane now has a national practice located in Tampa, representing some of America's most preeminent corporations in product liability defense matters as both national and local counsel. Diane's experience as a large-firm associate, partner, small-firm shareholder, and owner of a cooperative law practice makes her uniquely qualified to serve PeopleWealth's individual and law practice clients in retention and job satisfaction programs. She is an active member of the Florida Bar Quality of Life and Stress Management Committee, a principal in PeopleWealth, and a novelist. She lives with her husband, Robert, and their dog, Molly, in Tampa, Florida, and Traverse City, Michigan.

Lori-Ann has been practicing law for fourteen years. She moved from outside counsel to inside counsel when she took a job as corporate counsel with St. John Health System in 1993. Lori-Ann's responsibilities have grown with the institution, whose parent corporation is the largest Catholic health system in the country. Lori-Ann is now Senior Corporate Compliance Specialist in a department that is responsible for the compliance requirements of more than 20,000 employees and 2,500 physicians working for a billion-dollar institution. Her responsibilities have encompassed all the transactional aspects of running a large corporation, including all contract and real estate transactions, as well as compliance. Lori-Ann serves on the Michigan Bar Standing Committee on the Quality of Professional Life, and is also listed in *Who's Who*. Lori-Ann's experience as a large-firm associate, partner, and corporate counsel provides both unique and universal insights for PeopleWealth's clients. She is a principal in PeopleWealth and a single mother of two young daughters, Alyssa and Cassandra. Lori-Ann, the girls, and their vizsla, Cally, live in Grosse Pointe Farms, Michigan.

We are very interested in your comments, suggestions, and insights. At this time, we have not planned revised editions of this book, but we may write revisions when the additional information we gather and learn warrants. If you are interested in PeopleWealth's services or simply want to share your views on these subjects with us, please contact us at:

PeopleWealth
100 North Tampa Street
Suite 2100
Tampa, Florida 33602
Telephone: (813) 221-0091
Facsimile: (813) 221-8116
www.PeopleWealth.com

BIBLIOGRAPHY

Aaron, Deborah. *What Can You Do With A Law Degree?: A Lawyer's Guide to Career Alternatives Inside, Outside And Around The Law.* 4th ed. New York: Niche Press, 1999.

Aburdene, Patricia, and John Naisbitt. *Megatrends.* New York: Random House, 1992.

Baker, Debra. "Dream Weavers." *ABA Journal* (June 1998).

Beckwith, Harry. *Selling the Invisible.* New York: Warner, 1997.

Blanchard, Ken. *The One-Minute Manager.* Berkeley: William Morrow & Co., 1993.

Buckingham, Marcus, and Curt Coffman. *First, Break All The Rules: What The World's Greatest Managers Do Differently.* New York: Simon & Schuster, 1999.

Carlson, Ronald, Ph.D. *Don't Sweat the Small Stuff.* New York: Hyperion, 1997.

Catalyst Guide. *Advancing Women in Business.* San Francisco: Jossey-Bass, 1998.

Collins, James C., and Jerry I. Porras. *Built to Last: Successful Habits of Visionary Companies.* New York: HarperCollins, 1994.

Cook, Marshall J. *10-Minute Guide to Motivating People.* New York: CWL Publishing Enterprises, 1997.

Cotterman, James D. *Compensation Plans for Law Firms.* 2d ed. Chicago: ABA Law Practice Management Section, 1995.

Covey, Stephen R. *The Seven Habits of Highly Effective People.* New York: Simon & Schuster, 1989.

Csikszentmihalyi, Mihaly. *Flow.* New York: HarperCollins, 1990.

Dominguez, Joe, and Vicki Robin. *Your Money or Your Life.* New York: Penguin Books, 1992.

Edwards, Paul, et al. *Getting Business to Come to You.* New York: Tarcher Putnam, 1998.

Fisher, Roger, and William Ury. *Getting to Yes.* New York: Penguin Books, 1983.

Gerson, Richard F., Ph.D. *Marketing Strategies for Small Businesses.* Menlo Park, CA: Crisp Publications, 1994.

Goluboff, Nicole Belson. *Telecommuting for Lawyers.* Chicago: ABA Law Practice Management Section, 1998.

Greene, Arthur G. *Strengthening Your Firm: Strategies for Success.* Chicago: ABA Law Practice Management Section, 1997.

Gubman, Edward L., Ph.D. *The Talent Solution.* New York: McGraw-Hill, 1998.

Johnson, Spencer, and Ken Blanchard. *Who Moved My Cheese?* New York: Penguin Books, 1998.

Jones, Laurie Beth. *The Path.* New York: Hyperion, 1996.

Kaufman, George W. *The Lawyer's Guide to Balancing Life and Work.* Chicago: ABA Law Practice Management Section, 1999.

LeBoeuf, Michael, Ph.D. *How to Win Customers and Keep Them for Life.* New York: Berkeley Books, 1987.

Levering, Robert, and Milton Moskowitz. "The 100 Best Companies To Work For." *Fortune* (Jan. 12, 1998).

NALP Foundation for Research and Education. *Employing Associates in 1998: Patterns and Practices.* Washington, D.C.: NALP, 1998.

NALP Foundation for Research and Education. *Keeping the Keepers; Strategies for Associate Retention in Times of Attrition.* Washington, D.C.: NALP, 1998.

NALP Foundation for Research and Education. *Perceptions of Partnership: The Allure and Accessibility of the Brass Ring.* Washington, D.C.: NALP, 1999.

Nelson, Bob. *1001 Ways to Reward Employees.* New York: Workman Publishing, 1994.

Nossel, Suzanne, and Elizabeth Westfall. *Presumed Equal: What America's Top Women Lawyers Really Think About Their Firms.* Cambridge, MA: Harvard Women's Law Association, 1998.

Paulson, Terry L., Ph.D. *Paulson on Change.* Glendale, CA: Griffin Publishing, 1996.

Paulson, Terry L., Ph.D. *They Shoot Managers, Don't They?* Berkeley, CA: Ten Speed Press, 1991.

Peters, Tom. *The Pursuit of WOW!* New York: Vintage, 1994.

Poley, Michelle Fairfield. *A Winning Attitude: How to Develop Your Most Important Asset.* Mission, KS: SkillPath Publications, Inc., 1992.

Schein, Edgar H., *Organizational Culture and Leadership,* San Francisco: Jossey-Bass, 1997.

Sells, Benjamin. *The Soul of the Law.* Nashville, TN: Thomas Moore, 1994.

Senge, Peter. *The Dance of Change: The Challenges to Sustaining Momentum in Learning Organizations.* New York: Doubleday/Currency, 1999.

Shannon, Marcia P., and Manch, Susan G. *Recruiting Lawyers: How to Hire the Best Talent.* Chicago: ABA Law Practice Management Section, 1999.

Smart, Bradford D., Ph.D. *Topgrading: How Leading Companies Win by Hiring, Coaching and Keeping the Best People.* Paramus, N.J.: Prentice Hall, 1999.

Stewart, Thomas A. *Intellectual Capital.* New York: Doubleday, 1997.

Tulgan, Bruce. *Managing Generation X.* Santa Monica, CA: Merritt, 1995.

Wilson, Larry, and Hersch Wilson. *Play to Win!* Austin, TX: Bard Press, 1998.

Zey, Michael. *The Right Move: How to Find the Perfect Job.*

INDEX

Selected Books From . . .
THE ABA LAW PRACTICE MANAGEMENT SECTION

The ABA Guide to International Business Negotiations. Explains national, legal, and cultural issues you must consider when negotiating with members of different countries. Includes details of 17 specific countries/nationalities.

The ABA Guide to Lawyer Trust Accounts. Details ways that lawyers should manage trust accounts to comply with ethical & statutory requirements.

The ABA Guide to Legal Marketing. 14 articles—written by marketing experts, practicing lawyers, and law firm marketing administrators—share their innovative methods for competing in an aggressive marketplace.

The ABA Guide to Professional Managers in the Law Office. Shows how lawyers can practice more efficiently by delegating management tasks to professional managers.

Anatomy of a Law Firm Merger. Considering a merger? Here's a roadmap that shows how to: determine the costs/benefits of a merger, assess merger candidates, integrate resources and staff, and more.

Billing Innovations. Explains how billing and pricing are affect strategic planning, maintaining quality of services, marketing, instituting a compensation system, and firm governance.

Changing Jobs, 3rd Edition. A handbook designed to help lawyers make changes in their professional careers. Includes career planning advice from dozens of experts.

Compensation Plans for Law Firms, 2nd Ed. This second edition discusses the basics for a fair and simple compensation system for partners, of counsel, associates, paralegals, and staff.

The Complete Internet Handbook for Lawyers. A thorough orientation to the Internet, including e-mail, search engines, conducting research and marketing on the Internet, publicizing a Web site, Net ethics, security, viruses, and more. Features a updated, companion Web site with forms you can download and customize.

Computer-Assisted Legal Research: A Guide to Successful Online Searching. Covers the fundamentals of LEXIS®-NEXIS® and WESTLAW®, including practical information such as: logging on and off; formulating your search; reviewing results; modifying a query; using special features; downloading documents.

Computerized Case Management Systems. Thoroughly evaluates 35 leading case management software applications, helping you pick which is best for your firm.

Connecting with Your Client. Written by a psychologist, therapist, and legal consultant, this book presents communications techniques that will help ensure client cooperation and satisfaction.

Do-It-Yourself Public Relations. A hands-on guide (and diskette!) for lawyers with public relations ideas, sample letters, and forms.

Easy Self-Audits for the Busy Law Office. Dozens of evaluation tools help you determine what's working (and what's not) in your law office or legal department. You'll discover several opportunities for improved productivity and efficiency along the way!

Finding the Right Lawyer. Answers the questions people should ask when searching for legal counsel. Includes a glossary of legal specialties and the 10 questions to ask before hiring a lawyer.

Flying Solo: A Survival Guide for the Solo Lawyer, 2nd Ed. An updated guide to the issues unique to the solo practitioner.

Handling Personnel Issues in the Law Office. Packed with tips on "safely" and legally recruiting, hiring, training, managing, and terminating employees.

HotDocs® in One Hour for Lawyers. Offers simple instructions, ranging from generating a document from a template to inserting conditional text and creating custom dialogs.

How to Build and Manage an Employment Law Practice. Provides clear guidance and valuable tips for solo or small employment law practices, including preparation, marketing, accepting cases, and managing workload and finances. Includes several time-saving "fill in the blank" forms.

How to Build and Manage an Estates Law Practice. Provides the tools and guidance you'll need to start or improve an estates law practice, including

How to Build and Manage a Personal Injury Practice. Features all of the tactics, technology, and tools needed for a profitable practice, including hot to: write a sound business plan, develop a financial forecast, choose office space, market your practice, and more.

How to Draft Bills Clients Rush to Pay. Dozens of ways to draft bills that project honesty, competence, fairness and value.

How to Start and Build a Law Practice, Millennium 4th Edition. Jay Foonberg's classic guide has been completely updated and expanded! Features 128 chapters, including 30 new ones, that reveal secrets to successful planning, marketing, billing, client relations, and much more. Chock-full of forms, sample letters, and checklists, including a sample business plan, "The Foonberg Law Office Management Checklist," and more.

Internet Fact Finder for Lawyers. Shares all of the secrets, shortcuts, and realities of conducting research on the Net, including how to tap into Internet sites for investigations, depositions, and trial presentations.

Law Firm Partnership Guide: Getting Started. Examines the most important issues you must consider to ensure your partnership's success, including self-assessment, organization structure, written agreements, financing, and basic operations. Includes *A Model Partnership Agreement* on diskette.

Law Firm Partnership Guide: Strengthening Your Firm.
Addresses what to do after your firm is up and running, including
how to handle: change, financial problems, governance issues,
compensating firm owners, and leadership.

Law Law Law on the Internet. Presents the most influential law-
related Web sites. Features Web site reviews of the *National Law
Journal's 250*, so you can save time surfing the Net and quickly find
the information you need.

Law Office Policy and Procedures Manual, 3rd Ed. A model for
law office policies and procedures (includes diskette). Covers law
office organization, management, personnel policies, financial
management, technology, and communications systems.

Law Office Staff Manual for Solos and Small Firms. Use this
manual as is or customize it using the book's diskette. Includes
general office policies on confidentiality, employee compensation,
sick leave, sexual harassment, billing, and more.

The Lawyer's Guide to Creating Web Pages. A practical guide that
clearly explains HTML, covers how to design a Web site, and
introduces Web-authoring tools.

The Lawyer's Guide to the Internet. A guide to what the Internet
is (and isn't), how it applies to the legal profession, and the different
ways it can—and should—be used.

The Lawyer's Guide to Marketing on the Internet. This book
talks about the pluses and minuses of marketing on the Internet, as
well as how to develop an Internet marketing plan.

The Lawyer's Quick Guide to E-Mail. Covers basic and
intermediate topics, including setting up an e-mail program, sending
messages, managing received messages, using mailing lists, security,
and more.

**The Lawyer's Quick Guide to Microsoft® Internet Explorer; The
Lawyer's Quick Guide to Netscape® Navigator.** These two guides
de-mystify the most popular Internet browsers. Four quick and easy
lessons include: Basic Navigation, Setting a Bookmark, Browsing
with a Purpose, and Keeping What You Find.

The Lawyer's Quick Guide to Timeslips®. Filled with practical
examples, this guide uses three short, interactive lessons to show to
efficiently use Timeslips.

**The Lawyer's Quick Guide to WordPerfect® 7.0/8.0 for
Windows®.** Covers multitasking, entering and editing text,
formatting letters, creating briefs, and more. Includes a diskette with
practice exercises and word templates.

Leaders' Digest: A Review of the Best Books on Leadership. This
book will help you find the best books on leadership to help you
achieve extraordinary and exceptional leadership skills.

**Living with the Law: Strategies to Avoid Burnout and Create
Balance.** Examines ways to manage stress, make the practice of law
more satisfying, and improve client service.

Marketing Success Stories. This collection of anecdotes provides an
inside look at how successful lawyers market themselves, their
practice specialties, their firms, and their profession.

Microsoft® Word for Windows® in One Hour for Lawyers. Uses
four easy lessons to help you prepare, save, and edit a basic
document in Word.

Practicing Law Without Clients: Making a Living as a Freelan
Lawyer. Describes freelance legal researching, writing, and
consulting opportunities that are available to lawyers.

Quicken® in One Hour for Lawyers. With quick, concise
instructions, this book explains the basics of Quicken and how to
the program to detect and analyze financial problems.

Risk Management. Presents practical ways to asses your level of
risk, improve client services, and avoid mistakes that can lead to
costly malpractice claims, civil liability, or discipline. Includes L
Firm Quality/In Control (QUIC) Surveys on diskette and other to
to help you perform a self-audit.

Running a Law Practice on a Shoestring. Offers a crash course
successful entrepreneurship. Features money-saving tips on office
space, computer equipment, travel, furniture, staffing, and more.

Successful Client Newsletters. Written for lawyers, editors, write
and marketers, this book can help you to start a newsletter from
scratch, redesign an existing one, or improve your current practic
in design, production, and marketing.

Survival Guide for Road Warriors. A guide to using a noteboo
computer (laptop) and other technology to improve your product
in your office, on the road, in the courtroom, or at home.

Telecommuting for Lawyers. Discover methods for implementi
successful telecommuting program that can lead to increased
productivity, improved work product, higher revenues, lower
overhead costs, and better communications. Addressing both la
firms and telecommuters, this guide covers start-up, budgeting,
setting policies, selecting participants, training, and technology.

Through the Client's Eyes. Includes an overview of client rela
and sample letters, surveys, and self-assessment questions to gau
your client relations acumen.

Time Matters® in One Hour for Lawyers. Employs quick, ea
lessons to show you how to: add contacts, cases, and notes to Ti
Matters; work with events and the calendar; and integrate your o
into a case management system that suits your needs.

Wills, Trusts, and Technology. Reveals why you should autom
your estates practice; identifies what should be automated; expla
how to select the right software; and helps you get up and runni
with the software you select.

Win-Win Billing Strategies. Prepared by a blue-ribbon ABA t
force of practicing lawyers, corporate counsel, and management
consultants, this book explores what constitutes "value" and ho
bill for it. You'll understand how to get fair compensation for y
work and communicate and justify fees to cost-conscious client

Women Rainmakers' 101+ Best Marketing Tips. A collectio
over 130 marketing from women rainmakers throughout the co
Features tips on image, networking, public relations, and adver

Year 2000 Problem and the Legal Profession. In clear,
nontechnical terms, this book will help you identify, address, a
meet the challenges that Y2K poses to the legal industry.

Qty	Title	LPM Price	Regular Price	Total
____	ABA Guide to International Business Negotiations (5110331)	$ 74.95	$ 84.95	$_____
____	ABA Guide to Lawyer Trust Accounts (5110374)	69.95	79.95	$_____
____	ABA Guide to Legal Marketing (5110341)	69.95	79.95	$_____
____	ABA Guide to Prof. Managers in the Law Office (5110373)	69.95	79.95	$_____
____	Anatomy of a Law Firm Merger (5110310)	24.95	29.95	$_____
____	Billing Innovations (5110366)	124.95	144.95	$_____
____	Changing Jobs, 3rd Ed.	*please call for information*		$_____
____	Compensation Plans for Lawyers, 2nd Ed. (5110353)	69.95	79.95	$_____
____	Complete Internet Handbook for Lawyers (5110413)	39.95	49.95	$_____
____	Computer-Assisted Legal Research (5110388)	69.95	79.95	$_____
____	Computerized Case Management Systems (5110409)	39.95	49.95	$_____
____	Connecting with Your Client (5110378)	54.95	64.95	$_____
____	Do-It-Yourself Public Relations (5110352)	69.95	79.95	$_____
____	Easy Self Audits for the Busy Law Firm	*please call for information*		$_____
____	Finding the Right Lawyer (5110339)	14.95	14.95	$_____
____	Flying Solo, 2nd Ed. (5110328)	29.95	34.95	$_____
____	Handling Personnel Issues in the Law Office (5110381)	59.95	69.95	$_____
____	HotDocs® in One Hour for Lawyers (5110403)	29.95	34.95	$_____
____	How to Build and Manage an Employment Law Practice (5110389)	44.95	54.95	$_____
____	How to Build and Manage an Estates Law Practice	*please call for information*		$_____
____	How to Build and Manage a Personal Injury Practice (5110386)	44.95	54.95	$_____
____	How to Draft Bills Clients Rush to Pay (5110344)	39.95	49.95	$_____
____	How to Start & Build a Law Practice, Millennium Fourth Edition (5110415)	47.95	54.95	$_____
____	Internet Fact Finder for Lawyers (5110399)	34.95	39.95	$_____
____	Law Firm Partnership Guide: Getting Started (5110363)	64.95	74.95	$_____
____	Law Firm Partnership Guide: Strengthening Your Firm (5110391)	64.95	74.95	$_____
____	Law Law Law on the Internet (5110400)	34.95	39.95	$_____
____	Law Office Policy & Procedures Manual (5110375)	99.95	109.95	$_____
____	Law Office Staff Manual for Solos & Small Firms (5110361)	49.95	59.95	$_____
____	Lawyer's Guide to Creating Web Pages (5110383)	54.95	64.95	$_____
____	Lawyer's Guide to the Internet (5110343)	24.95	29.95	$_____
____	Lawyer's Guide to Marketing on the Internet (5110371)	54.95	64.95	$_____
____	Lawyer's Quick Guide to E-Mail (5110406)	34.95	39.95	$_____
____	Lawyer's Quick Guide to Microsoft Internet® Explorer (5110392)	24.95	29.95	$_____
____	Lawyer's Quick Guide to Netscape® Navigator (5110384)	24.95	29.95	$_____
____	Lawyer's Quick Guide to Timeslips® (5110405)	34.95	39.95	$_____
____	Lawyer's Quick Guide to WordPerfect® 7.0/8.0 (5110395)	34.95	39.95	$_____
____	Leaders' Digest (5110356)	49.95	59.95	$_____
____	Living with the Law (5110379)	59.95	69.95	$_____
____	Marketing Success Stories (5110382)	79.95	89.95	$_____
____	Microsoft® Word for Windows® in One Hour for Lawyers (5110358)	19.95	29.95	$_____
____	Practicing Law Without Clients (5110376)	49.95	59.95	$_____
____	Quicken® in One Hour for Lawyers (5110380)	19.95	29.95	$_____
____	Risk Management (5610123)	69.95	79.95	$_____
____	Running a Law Practice on a Shoestring (5110387)	39.95	49.95	$_____
____	Successful Client Newsletters (5110396)	39.95	44.95	$_____
____	Survival Guide for Road Warriors (5110362)	24.95	29.95	$_____
____	Telecommuting for Lawyers (5110401)	39.95	49.95	$_____
____	Through the Client's Eyes (5110337)	69.95	79.95	$_____
____	Time Matters® in One Hour for Lawyers (5110402)	29.95	34.95	$_____
____	Wills, Trusts, and Technology (5430377)	74.95	84.95	$_____
____	Win-Win Billing Strategies (5110304)	89.95	99.95	$_____
____	Women Rainmakers' 101+ Best Marketing Tips (5110336)	14.95	19.95	$_____
____	Year 2000 Problem and the Legal Profession (5110410)	24.95	29.95	$_____

Handling

$10.00-$24.99....................$3.95
$25.00-$49.99....................$4.95
$50.00+$5.95   MD residents add 5%

Tax

DC residents add 5.75%
IL residents add 8.75%

Subtotal	$_____
*Handling	$_____
**Tax	$_____
TOTAL	$_____

PAYMENT

☐ Check enclosed (to the ABA) ☐ Bill Me
☐ Visa ☐ MasterCard ☐ American Express

Account Number _____ Exp. Date _____ Signature _____

Name _____ Firm _____

Address _____

City _____ State _____ Zip _____

Phone Number _____ E-Mail Address _____

Mail: ABA Publication Orders, P.O. Box 10892, Chicago, Illinois 60610-0892 ♦ Phone: (800) 285-2221 ♦ FAX: (312) 988-5568

E-Mail: abasvcctr@abanet.org ♦ Internet: http://www.abanet.org/lpm/catalog

Source Code: 22AEND499

 **THE SECTION OF LAW PRACTICE MANAGEMENT**

CUSTOMER COMMENT FORM

Title of Book:_____

We've tried to make this publication as useful, accurate, and readable as possible. Please take 5 minutes to tell us if we succeeded. Your comments and suggestions will help us improve our publications. Thank you!

1. How did you acquire this publication:

☐ by mail order   ☐ at a meeting/convention   ☐ as a gift

☐ by phone order   ☐ at a bookstore   ☐ don't know

☐ other: (describe) _____

Please rate this publication as follows:

	Excellent	Good	Fair	Poor	Not Applicable
Readability: Was the book easy to read and understand?	☐	☐	☐	☐	☐
Examples/Cases: Were they helpful, practical? Were there enough?	☐	☐	☐	☐	☐
Content: Did the book meet your expectations? Did it cover the subject adequately?	☐	☐	☐	☐	☐
Organization and clarity: Was the sequence of text logical? Was it easy to find what you wanted to know?	☐	☐	☐	☐	☐
Illustrations/forms/checklists: Were they clear and useful? Were there enough?	☐	☐	☐	☐	☐
Physical attractiveness: What did you think of the appearance of the publication (typesetting, printing, etc.)?	☐	☐	☐	☐	☐

Would you recommend this book to another attorney/administrator? ☐ Yes ☐ No

How could this publication be improved? What else would you like to see in it?

_____
_____
_____

Do you have other comments or suggestions? _____
_____
_____

Name _____
Firm/Company _____
Address _____
City/State/Zip _____
Phone _____
Firm Size: _____ Area of specialization: _____

We appreciate your time and help.

Fold

BUSINESS REPLY MAIL
FIRST CLASS   PERMIT NO. 16471   CHICAGO, ILLINOIS

POSTAGE WILL BE PAID BY ADDRESSEE

AMERICAN BAR ASSOCIATION
PPM, 8th FLOOR
750 N. LAKE SHORE DRIVE
CHICAGO, ILLINOIS 60611–9851

Fold

AMERICAN BAR ASSOCIATION

Membership Application

Law Practice Management Section

Access to all these information resources and discounts – for just $3.33 a month!

Membership dues are just $40 a year – just $3.33 a month.
You probably spend more on your general business magazines and newspapers.
But they can't help you succeed in building and managing your practice
like a membership in the ABA Law Practice Management Section.
Make a small investment in success. Join today!

☑ **Yes!**   **I want to join the ABA Section of Law Practice Management Section** and gain access to information helping me add more clients, retain and expand business with current clients, and run my law practice more efficiently and competitively!

Check the dues that apply to you:

❑ $40 for ABA members   ❑ $5 for ABA Law Student Division members

Choose your method of payment:

❑ Check enclosed (make payable to American Bar Association)
❑ Bill me
❑ Charge to my: ❑ VISA®   ❑ MASTERCARD®   ❑ AMEX®

Card No.: _____   Exp. Date: _____

Signature: _____   Date: _____

ABA I.D.*: _____
(∗ *Please note: Membership in ABA is a prerequisite to enroll in ABA Sections.*)

Name: _____

Firm/Organization: _____

Address: _____

City/State/ZIP: _____

Telephone No.: _____   Fax No.: _____

Primary Email Address: _____

Get Ahead. 🏃

/ABA Law Practice Management Section

**Save time
by Faxing
or Phoning!**
AMERICAN BAR ASSOCIATION

750 N. LAKE SHORE DRIVE
CHICAGO, IL 60611
PHONE: (312) 988-5619
FAX: (312) 988-5820
Email: lpm@abanet.org

▶ Fax your application to: (312) 988-5820
▶ Join by phone if using a credit card: (800) 285-2221 (ABA1)
▶ Email us for more information at: lpm@abanet.org
▶ Check us out on the Internet: http://www.abanet.org/lpm

I understand that Section dues include a $24 basic subscription to Law Practice Management; this subscription charge is not deductible from the dues and additional subscriptions are not available at this rate. Membership dues in the American Bar Association are not deductible as charitable contributions for income tax purposes. However, such dues may be deductible as a business expense.